The red velvet seat

{ a memoir }

BARRY D. YOUNG

Redbrush

#082017

THIS BOOK IS 100 PERCENT BARRY YOUNG, not just the present-day Barry, but the little kid Barry I watched grow up. The Barry who always walked with a smile on his face, who was always polite and gracious. The Barry who always could make you smile (Mr. Personality). The Barry who came from good stock, who got the right stuff poured into him... I'm saying all this to say your book is an extension of you, the evolved Barry who transitioned into manhood gracefully. I find your book a very refreshing read, it's very organic and honest... The people who traveled with you for those thirty years will smile, laugh and cry as they recall those historic moments... I give your book a 10... Thumps up... Love you Bro. B...

--Jonathan Lewis
Recording artist and founding member of
Atlantic Starr

TABLE OF CONTENTS

TABLE OF CONTENTS (CONT'D.)

DEDICATION

With great love to my twelve siblings:

Michael Toney McCrimmon
Pat Williams McCrimmon
Anita McCrimmon
Aretha McCrimmon
April Addison
Dennis McCrimmon
Debbie Byrd McCrimmon
Timothy Jarvis McCrimmon
Anthony McCrimmon
Garrpatrick McCrimmon
Jason McCrimmon
Alice McCrimmon
Seth Vanderberg

To my Mother:
Sue Theola Young
whom I love and miss

and my Father:
Garfemia McCrimmon
whom I love and finally understand

F O R E W O R D

Ⅰ FIRST ENCOUNTERED BARRY YOUNG on an 8:41 train out of Grand Central heading toward White Plains, New York. Morning trains are usually pretty quiet, as most commuters are still awakening from too little sleep the night before or texting their way into another day. But I'd become aware some months ago of a particular conductor who had a gift for bringing cheer into our mundane trip to work. That was Barry.

I'd been riding the train long enough to observe the demeanor of various conductors. Some were pleasant enough. For others, it was clearly just a job. However, no one engaged the passengers like Barry. He called us by nicknames. He told stories. And in stark contrast to the majority of those present, he actually seemed happy to be there, grateful for another day, doing his level best to welcome strangers and convert those strangers into friends.

Life here is often hard, and New York City commuters develop a thick skin over time. It protects us from the knocks you get in a large urban environment. But it can also form a protective shell that keeps even the good things from penetrating. Barry was the guy who managed to get under our skins in a good way, bringing us closer by reminding us of our humanity. Without him, we were so many droids mechanically going to and fro. With Barry, the dull ride took on a shine.

The Red Velvet Seat is a celebration of a life well-lived. Barry's book traces the values and experiences that shaped him from childhood, chronicles many of his passions and stands as a prophecy for his future, because that 'life well-lived' is far from over.

Before official work began on this book, Barry invited me to Grand Central last October for his final day of work, the last ride he would make into that famous terminal. I arrived early, not knowing what to expect. Would there be a ceremony? Would the Chairman of the Railroad make a speech against a background of patriotic bunting, strapping a gold watch on the retiring man's wrist?

What actually happened bested even my writer's imagination. There was no band or bunting, but as soon as the train came to rest and the doors opened, a spontaneous receiving line began forming on the platform. Dozens of passengers with cards, gifts and flowers in hand got in the queue to thank their conductor and wish him the best in the next chapter of his life.

I've seen plenty of things in my life that moved me deeply, but that scene ranks in the top three. It was clear in that moment that it had never been merely a job for Barry Young. It was his ministry.

There's a time in every man's life when he needs to tell his story. I consider myself lucky and exceedingly blessed that Barry chose me to help him tell his.

– Mark E. Lanham, October 2016

INTRODUCTION

O N THE MORNING of October 30, 2015 at about 8:30, I rode my Metro North Harlem Line train into Manhattan's famed Grand Central Terminal for the last time. After thirty-three years–a career that be-gan with me taking trash out of the same cars that later be-came the stage for my own *Daily Show*–I was hanging it up. It was the day before Halloween, and I was wearing a black Phan-tom of the Opera mask. I never missed out on an opportunity to entertain the troops.

The mask covered half my face, but it couldn't have con-cealed my joy as folks who rode with me for years spilled out onto the platform, wishing me well in the next chapter of my life. Many of them knew I had a pretty big bucket list to fulfill, and by God's grace I was hoping I'd get to most of it. Taking my grandsons fishing was at the top of the list.

Reflecting now on those thirty-three years, I see how my conductor job was an intensive three-decade course in learning not to judge. The daily act of meeting strangers, greeting the public and being of service in the closed environment of a fast-moving train taught me things about myself and human nature that no other job could, in my humble opinion. Being honest, I will tell you that where I started out that ride is a long way from where I ended up—and hence the story.

The Red Velvet Seat is a symbol of authority. Anyone who has ever sat there understands the assignments that come along with it: humility, love and understanding the plight of the common man. You can use or abuse the Red Velvet Seat. This book tracks my journey learning to respect it, not abuse it. With every mile, I understood that God's grace and mercy had put me in that seat in the first place. The better choice was to see it as the perfect place from which to love, not judge. For me, it became the position to dispense something beyond tickets--an abundance of love to anyone in need.

The world is full of judgment. So full, in fact, that violence over race, religion, class, education, and even standing room on a train has become an everyday happening. More often than any other factor, it is judgement that moves us to violence—to use harsh words, to raise our fist, to pick up a gun in order to settle the score.

Not all judgment is bad. We need *good* judgment in order to survive. Judging people and situations accurately is how we navigate our way through life and avoid pain. If I judge that a parking space is too short for my vehicle, I avoid the pain of trying to wedge myself in there. (Luckily, I drive a Fiat 500, so I usually don't have that issue.)

The judgments I'm addressing are the ones which put us either above or below the person we're dealing with. As a conductor walking the aisles, I was in a posture where I had to look down at my passengers. However, when I learned not to look down *on* them, regardless of who they were or how they treated me, the daily ride became fun for everyone.

Two things happen when we make the choice not to judge people. We discover that what we have in common outweighs our differences. And when that becomes our reality, life becomes a big dance party–a kaleidoscopic, multi-colored event where we all pile out onto the dance floor and groove to the same beat.

I invite you to take this journey with me, a trip that recalls some of the most memorable episodes of my life–funny, serious and everything in-between–and how those experiences taught me to stop judging others and start dancing. As a kid who grew up watching *Soul Train*, the dance metaphor is a powerful one for me. In fact, at my retirement party back in November, once the music started I never left the dance floor. I hope I never do.

Here's my other hope—that these stories will cause you to look at the way you judge people and situations, and maybe flip the script on yourself as I did. My course took thirty-three years. Maybe by reading this, your trip will be a little shorter. So get your feet ready. The music is about to begin.

B.D.Y. – *January 2016*

PLAYING
WITH FIRE

Kids OFTEN MISJUDGE. People, situations, anything. One of my earliest memories of this was a particular Saturday when my cousin Earl and I were spending the night with Popie, my grandfather, at their house, 52 Maryton Road in White Plains, New York. You'll hear me refer often to the Maryton Road house, because at that time, it was the epicenter of activity for the Young family.

Popie had told us to go to bed. *He* was going to bed. We had church the next morning, and had to be up early to all get on our knees in the living room and pray before Grandma served up her generous breakfast of waffles, pancakes, homemade syrup, bacon, sausage and grits. My grandmother was a whiz in the kitchen. Her real name was Helen Howcott Young, but she became "Lala" after the baby of a rich Scarsdale family she worked for gave her that nickname. The baby's parents were trying to get their child to say "Helen," but what came out of the baby's mouth was "Lala," and it stuck.

My grandfather wasn't much of a disciplinarian. That role was fulfilled for the Young family by my mother's middle sister, Rev. Eloise L. Young. She wasn't yet using the "Dr." in front of her name, but she was already a fiery preacher in the Pentecostal tradition, and regularly held forth at Saint James F.B.H. Church. The F.B.H. stood for "Fire-Baptised Holiness," and anyone who heard Aunt Weezie preach was sure to get a little singed around the edges. Needless to say, her Christian convictions enabled her to deliver a solid whipping when the situation called for it. But Popie was more of a soft touch. On that night, he had clearly told us to go to bed, but Earl and I judged that our time would be better spent playing a little nighttime Nok Hockey downstairs.

Kids always think that they can outsmart adults. My cousin and I figured that Popie would soon be snoring away, and if he happened to wake up, we'd hear him in time to beat it back upstairs to our own room before he could emerge from his bedroom. Well sure enough, in mid-game we heard him stirring around, but miscalculated the timing of our escape. As we dashed back up the stairs in the dark, Earl's waist-high head ran smack into Popie's stomach, bounced off and my cousin landed on the floor, flat on his back. "What were you boys doing down there?!" Popie fussed. "I thought I told you to go to bed!" At that point, I couldn't tell whether Earl was laughing or crying. My grandfather never hit us–that was Aunt Weezie's job. And she was about to get to it.

It happened one day when I was about eight. I was coming home from basketball practice to our Maryton Road house when I encountered Scotty Leach, another one of my cousins, who was out front. Scotty was five at the time, and already an exact replica of Uncle Teddy, my mother's twin brother–had his walk, talked like him, the whole package. Scotty was also a mischievous little dude.

As I approached, I saw that my little cousin had whipped out his wiener and was about to pee on the big tree in Lala and Popie's front lawn. Taking the law into my own hands, I immediately ran in the house and proudly announced to my aunt and grandmother that Scotty was peeing on the front lawn.

Right behind me, Scotty ran in the house and just as quickly countered my accusation. "So what?!" he began excitedly, tucking himself back into his pants. "*So what* if I was peeing on the lawn. *You* guys were downstairs playing with matches and lighting cigarettes."

That really got Aunt Weezie's attention. "What?! What do you mean?!" she demanded. Seeing his quickness of wit had gotten the attention off of his own behavior, Scotty offered, "C'mon, I got the *evidence*!" Even at five, my cousin knew an accusation like that demanded proof. He'd spat out the word "evidence" like a budding district attorney. "I can show you the matches and cigarettes and *everything*!" And smiling a mischievous smile, Scotty led the parade downstairs to my Aunt Carolyn's apartment.

Aunt Carol smoked, and as we all know, where there's smoke, there's bound to be fire. It was down there where Cousin Earl and I, along with my two older female cousins Lori and Shaun would light cigarettes and try taking little puffs–like we were sophisticated adults–along with lighting some candles. When we arrived at the scene of the crime, the evidence was all over the place–dozens of burned matches, candles and a crumpled, half-empty pack of Aunt Carolyn's Virginia Slims Menthols.

We all stood looking at each other as the gravity of the situation sunk in. Lala and Aunt Weezie were clearly recalling every newspaper article they'd read in the last fifteen years about unattended kids lighting matches and burning down houses and apartment buildings. *Me and my big mouth*, I thought to myself, wishing I'd kept Scotty's peeing to myself, kept my big mouth shut and gone into the house and grabbed some Kool Aid instead. We knew what was coming next, so might as well get it over with. Earl and I blurted out our confessions and apologized with all the sincerity we could manage. We knew it wouldn't help, but it was all we could do. Even Johnny Cochran couldn't have helped us at that point.

Aunt Weezie's ritual for administering corporal punishment was well-known. She marched us back upstairs and lined us up at the bathroom door while she sat on the edge of the tub. Then, using her knees like a vise, she'd clamp our heads between them and beat down on top of us. Earl and I took it like men. The rest had lied their way out of it and avoided punishment.

It wasn't the first, nor would it be the last time I came under the firm hand of Aunt Weezie's correctional rehabilitation program. This one, however, made a lasting impression. I saw that Scotty's offense was forgivable, given his age. More than that, how did *I* know that he hadn't been waiting for somebody to get out of the bathroom in the house, and chose the yard only when he believed he had no other option? I could wish that he'd at least have chosen the *back* yard, but that wasn't the point. The point was that I had issues in my own back yard that came to light (and got me a whipping) because I was in such a rush to judge my little cousin. Like the Scripture says, I was so interested in taking that little splinter out of Scotty's eye that I ended up tripping over the log in my own.

STANDING
IN THE NEED

"JUDGE NOT." Most church people can also give you the other half of that verse, from Jesus' Sermon on the Mount: "...that ye be not judged." (KJV) So why then are some of the most judgmental folks I've met *church people*? I still try to wrap my mind around that one. My own spiritual journey stretches from childhood up through one of the darkest places in my life to the present. It's the chapter of my life where I learned about what I now call "religious judgmentalism." It taught me a plain truth: that judgment never saved anybody. What saves is love.

Church was a ritual for as long as I can remember. When I was a kid living at my grandmother's home on Maryton Road, preparation for Sunday church actually began on Saturday night.

If I asked to go to a party Friday evening, there would be less resistance than if I asked for Saturday night. If I stayed out late Friday, the downside was I still had to do my chores before I could watch *Soul Train*. But if I went out Saturday, this was the ultimatum. I can still hear Grandmother's words in my ears, "I don't care *how* late you stay out, *everyone* in this house gets up for church come Sunday morning."

First there was Sunday school, and then came church. My grandmother's church–the Fire-Baptised Holiness congregation–was a strict religion. However, I found out I didn't know from strict until my aunt came along. She followed a preacher out of Queens named Johnny Washington, *Apostle* Johnny Apostle, and they were part of the Pentecostal movement. And they were stricter than strict.

Lala, my grandmother, was a God-fearing woman. But she never judged people. When the Pentecostals came around, however, it was a whole different deal. If you didn't do what Pastor Johnny did, you got judged. If you didn't make your kids go to church as much as Apostle Johnny's members were made to go to church, you got judged. If you had a child out of wedlock, it was likely that people wouldn't speak to you. They weren't God–any of them, but my feeling was that they were sure good at playing Him.

It was all no-nonsense at Pastor Johnny's Tabernacle of

Prayer. He'd been a gospel singer back in the 1960s with a group called the Gospel Wonders. I can understand why things were the way they were. Before they turned around, they had led lives that may have been somewhat sinful, and they wanted people to turn around as they had done. But the force of it was still judgmental to me. You had to be at prayer meeting at eight o'clock. If you weren't, your name did not get on the list. If your name was not on the list, you could not hold a church office. And that was that.

Dancing was another basis for judgment–but it all depended on the location. Aunt Weezie used to preach against people "goin' to boogaloo." That's what she called dancing–boogaloo. Around Lala's house when I'd play certain records, she'd shout at me, "Turn that boogaloo music down!" But it was a double-edged sword, because in church, if you *weren't* dancing in praise of the Lord, she'd call you out. "Why aren't y'all dancing?! Let's get it going! You act like y'all don't love the Lord!" How she could come to that conclusion?! But she wasn't done yet. "Some of you act like you can't praise the Lord today," she'd continue. "Y'all was out boogalooin' last night, huh?" Dancing to James Brown on a Saturday night was a sin; *not* dancing on Sunday morning was a sin. It wasn't logical, but they didn't care. They made the rules. Judge and jury. From my immature point of view, that's what I thought.

It made me angry, too, that there seemed to be a double standard. There's a little verse in the Bible that says when pastors or anointed people do things, you as a congregant aren't allowed to say anything. "Touch not mine anointed, and do my prophets no harm," it says in 1 Chronicles 16:22. That kept people quiet about what they saw and allowed, among other things, the abuse of children in many churches to go on for a long, long time.

It also angered me that I got judged by what things looked like, without people knowing what was in my heart. One case involved me doing what seemed like a good thing–getting my friends from the projects to come to church with me. One of them was a guy named Spanky.

Spanky was an older guy who wasn't doing too well in life, but I loved him as a guy who'd always been good to me. One Sunday before service, I drove over by his place. Leaning out of the car window, I said, "C'mon, Spanky, come to church with me today!" He paused. "Aw Barry, you *know* I don't have nothin' to wear to church," he said, looking down at his clothes. "And look how fine *you're* dressed." I tried to persuade him, but it was clear that he wasn't going with me. Eventually I drove off, but I had a plan.

Next Sunday I was back. "C'mon, Spanky, come to church with me today!" Spanky looked at me. "There you are *again*, Barry. You're playin' with me," he said. I parked the car and jumped out. "Look at my feet," I said as Spanky eyed me up and down. This time I wore jeans, a T-shirt and sneakers—same as him. "*Now* will you come?!" I pleaded. Spanky gave me a long song and look and smiled. "Okay, Barry, that was a good one. You got me that time. But I still can't go—got no money for the offering." I took a five dollar bill out of my pocket. "Here's five for the offering. *Now* will you come with me?" But Spanky waved the bill away and eyed the ground. "Sorry, B, I'm not going to go today."

I got back in the car and drove to church, telling God as I drove along, "Well, I did my best." At church that morning, it was the usual deal. Aunt Weezie's preaching could easily go on for three or four hours. And that wasn't Scripture reading. That was just her, giving her take on things. At one point she abruptly turned toward me and announced to the congregation, "And look at my nephew Barry, comin' up in here in a *T-shirt* and *sneakers* for shoes!"

Today, I can't remember if I answered her right then and there or later, but I had to say something. I wasn't humiliated by what she'd said; my spirit was stronger than that. But I told her straight-up. "Aunt Weezie," I began, "I know you've been preaching for a long time. I may not be a holy roller in your book, but I have a strong relationship with God. I'm dressed like this because I was trying to get one of my friends from the projects to come to church with me this morning. When I tried with him on last week, he said he couldn't come to church because he didn't have the right clothes. I wore this when I went back today to make him feel better about coming in his own jeans and sneakers–told him it didn't matter."

What hurt most is that she had misjudged me. She looked at my appearance on that particular Sunday and she judged me. I told her later, "You have no idea what God is doing in my heart– what me and God are doing. He doesn't tell you everything. You may *think* He does, but He doesn't."

I believe that God has given Man just a little bit of knowledge about what His thoughts are in order to see what we'll do with that God-inspired Scripture. He didn't give us the whole thing, because we wouldn't be able to handle it. And look what we've done with it. Hundreds of religions that wall us up in smaller and smaller groups, centuries of religious wars–all that killing done in the name of God or Allah or whoever. Probably not what He had in mind.

My feelings have been stronger on this as I've gotten older. I watched people in the church talk about other people. And I'm saying, "Where's God in *that*?" Church people turned down invitations to my retirement party because we served liquor and had dancing. The party wasn't *religious* in their eyes. But those same people will go to church and look sideways at Sister So-

And-So and talk mean about her hat.

If the four-hour sermons weren't my favorite part of church, gospel music was. My all-time favorite gospel group is the Reverend Nat Townsley Jr. and the Tabernacle Lighthouse Choir from Brooklyn. As a kid who technically wasn't even saved at the time, I used to play their *I Fell in Love with God* album all the time, pulling it out of the stack of records that belonged to Aunt Weezie.

Another gospel song–John P. Kee's *Standing In The Need of Prayer*–guided me through the lowest point in my life. In 1991, I got in trouble with substance abuse–trouble that got me sent to rehab for thirty days until I was clean and could get my job back. Many people will tell you that you don't really encounter God until you're in that low valley. I don't know if it's true for everybody, but it was for me. I remember going into the secret closet of my room and crying out to God. I cried out for direction. I cried out for healing–for my mind, my body and my spirit.

Part of my crying out was that John P. Kee song. Some of the lyric goes *It's not my Aunt Bessie, it's not my Aunt So-And-So...* I would personalize those lyrics to *It's not my Aunt Weezie, but it's me, Lord, I'm Standing in the Need of Prayer.* In my darkest hours, I'd sing that song over and over until I was at peace. And I got a breakthrough. Maybe after many months, or just felt like months, but one thing was certain. Outside the organized religion that I'd grown up, the church that often said one thing and did another, I'd finally met the real God. Whatever doubt my previous religious experience might have cast upon His existence, I doubted no more. God was real. I'd been through a great trouble, but now I'd come through. For the first time in months, I felt like dancing. And that first dance was for the Lord.

There are some ironies in my spiritual journey. I saw a lot of judgment going on. I was misjudged. But I also misjudged others, including my own grandmother, Lala. The way she used to pray out loud made me uncomfortable. Whether in the house or at church, she had this way of crying out to God that annoyed me. I believed in her wisdom, but still I used to ask her, "Why do you have to scream and pray so loud?!" Her reply was always, "Oh, be *quiet*, boy–that's the way it is." Only after all this time have I realized that her loud praying that used to get under my skin was for me. I know I came through some of the things God's pulled me through and am intact today because of the prayers of my grandmother.

Not just me, either–I believe that a lot of her children experienced good lives because of her constant prayer. My grandparents didn't have a lot of money. Lala cleaned rich folks' houses in Scarsdale. Popie delivered coal for thirty years to heat those Scarsdale houses. They pulled together a comfortable living that supported their seven children, and also benefitted the twelve grandchildren that came along after that.

Spinning those prayers was a sign of my grandmother's constant devotion to me. I was the first grandchild she took in under her roof. My mother was having a rough time in the world, so the family felt it was better if I stayed with my grandmother. Sometimes I longed to go back to my mother, probably because I knew I'd be able to get away with things that Lala wouldn't have allowed.

I thank God for my Uncle Teddy. He passed recently, but I still call up his wife Mary and thank her for what Teddy did for me. If he hadn't put his foot down, jacked me up and pulled me by the collar a couple times, I would've been living back with my mother and hanging out with my friends in the other neighborhood, who were slightly more mischievous than the people in my grandmother's neighborhood.

My grandmother told it like it was. When I was mischievous, she would look at me in those high-water pants of mine and say, "Barry, you better cut this out–otherwise you're going to grow up to be a nobody." The truth often hurts, but I took it to heart. In my head, I though, "Oh my god–growing up to be a *nobody*... that's terrible!" But it kept me on track, and years later when I faced challenges at work, having to answer to officials for things they knew the passenger was lying about, I was able to keep my head up. Every time I met and overcame a challenge, I'd smile to myself and quietly say, "And here they said I was going to be a *nobody*..."

I won't lie: all my life I struggled to be a good boy. That mischievous nature is in me still. Thanks to my grandmother's prayers, however, the mischief I engage in now is harmless compared to how it could have gone down for me. Today, that mischievousness shows up when I joke with my friends. But in that case, it's all about fun—not negative 'ghetto' fun at someone else's expense, just fun. We laugh and laugh. "A cheerful heart is good medicine," says Proverbs 17:22. I try to get a laugh in every day—even if it's at myself. I have no problem with that.

Along the way I realized, too, that when it comes to prayer, everyone has to find their own way. Lala's crying out to the Lord used to get to me, but look what it did for her family. For me, prayer worked better as a private thing—me alone in my secret closet getting in touch with God. When I began to experience that connection, He started to put stuff in my heart. My God doesn't talk to me like a regular person; it's not like I'm hearing a ghost or anything. What He says to me is not even audible—it goes straight into my heart.

In my heart, I know that the church God has in mind has no walls. It exists as much outside the walls of Apostle Johnny Washington's Tabernacle of Prayer as it does within. It exists in rough neighborhoods where people wear sneakers on Sunday, haven't a dime for the collection, and stay away from church because they believe in their hearts that they wouldn't fit in. It even exists on a dance floor with James Brown playing on a Saturday night. Sorry, Aunt Weezie.

IT COULD
HAPPEN TO YOU

THINGS ARE NOT always as they appear. It's a lesson I learned on the train more than a few times–that what you see is not always what you get. Our eyes can really deceive us about people and situations. The more I learned to step back, give it a minute and not jump to conclusions, the more I began to see things as they really were.

Working around a large metropolitan area like Manhattan, you see a lot of things–people living on the edge, in survival mode. Jesus says in Mark 14:7 that the poor will always be with us. And if I had trusted my eyes, that's how I would have judged one guy who got on my train every day: disheveled, wild hair, clothes unkempt. I remember the first time I saw him, and how my immediate reaction was, "Oh boy, here we go..."

There's a way that people who get on a train with no fare will try to play you if you're the conductor. They fumble in their pockets, pretend to be searching for a ticket or some cash that never turns out to be there. That's exactly what I expected from this guy as I approached him. To my amazement, however, he not only produced a ticket from his pocket, but a monthly ticket that costs almost two hundred dollars. Now, I was like, "Whoa, are you kidding me?!"

After I found out this guy was legit, I watched other conductors judge as I had judged. They'd see this guy get on, and would walk down the car, nod toward him and say to me, "Barry, we got one on here–" meaning they thought we were going to have to put this guy off the train. I then saw the same surprise come across their faces that came across mine when he pulled that monthly ticket from his pocket.

That passenger turned out to be the nicest guy. I was never sure whether maybe he had some mental issue that would explain his appearance. Our conversations weren't long, and consisted mostly of "Good morning." But he was a pleasant guy, and I thank him from the bottom of my heart because he taught me that I just had to love everybody, and not judge things until I've seen the whole story. When I saw him that first time, fumbling for his ticket, I was ready to show him off the train. However, he showed me, and I thank God for it.

Lest we think that God doesn't have a sense of humor, our judgment has a funny way of looping back to us, just as it did on me when I ratted out Scotty for peeing on the lawn. This case involves another 'regular,' a homeless girl who used to show up on my train on a regular basis.

I'd guess that her heritage was Italian. Her face was severely pock-marked. She was the sweetest lady, though. Clearly she had fallen on hard times, and I had no doubt that she was on drugs of some kind. Her sole purpose for being on the train was to beg for money. And as much as I felt for her and her situation, we have rules against that kind of thing. Not my rules, but rules I had to follow. So I would walk up to her–and by now we were familiar with each other–and say, "C'mon, sweetheart, you know you can't do that. I have to ask you to leave." I wasn't nasty about it–there was no need to be. And she'd always say back to me, "Okay, yeah, I saw you coming." And I'd say, "Thank you."

One of my coworkers, a Puerto Rican guy named Luis, was less generous in his treatment of this girl. While my style was to politely ask her to leave, Luis' way was to say, "Get the f--- off this train, you scuzzbucket!" When I called him out on it, he immediately shot back, "Man, I am *tired* of her! She's always down here on this train, begging for money!"–as if that was somehow her preference on how she spent her day. "Hold up, man," I told him. "You don't have to talk to her that way, dude. That is not cool."

But Luis wasn't giving in. "What do you mean, Barry?" he said, irritated. I replied, "All you have to do is ask her to leave. You don't have to humiliate her." He contradicted me, "Yeah, but she is the scum of the earth. She's living on the streets, doing God-knows-what with her body..." I held up my hand. "Brother, I'm not going to preach to you, but the bottom line is that even you and I are only two or three mistakes away from being in her shoes. You don't need to act like that. You're a grown man. You've *got* a job."

I never knew if any of that sank in. What I do know is that one week after I called Luis out for treating her that way, he was fired for taking a customer's check out of another conductor's locker and trying to cash it at the ticket remittance office. We didn't get personal checks much on the train, but at one time we were allowed to accept them. Luis had taken one of those checks from somebody's locker and tried to cash it. They caught the whole thing on camera.

Some people would say he got what he deserved. I stop short of that, because I know, as a spiritual person, that we have all fallen short of the grace of God–*all* of us. A couple of mistakes and I could have been the one on that train asking for money. As

I write this, I wonder whatever happened to Luis. Did he learn from his mistake? I guess I'll never know. What I do know is that what you dish out has a funny way of coming back to you. And whatever crazy state you see somebody in, just remember that, as Ol' Blue Eyes used to croon, *"It Could Happen To You."*

HE'S GONNA
WORK IT OUT

HONOR YOUR FATHER. Those words still ring in my ears, even though my own father passed in 2004. Garfenia MᶜCrimmon was his name. He had me with my mother, Sue Theola Young, when they were not married, and when she was quite young. I always loved my dad's first name. There was something special about it. It fit, because he was a one-of-a-kind character. Different. Unique. Creative.

Garfenia MᶜCrimmon worked as a machine operator making rack and pinion systems for Chrysler Motor Company in Detroit. He was also on a journey, fathering thirteen children with six different women. Then as now, I'm sure there was a lot of judgment leveled at him for that. I was the first of those thirteen children, and had my issues with him, too. When I was young, I spent a fair amount of time wondering why my cousins' fathers were around and mine wasn't.

That judgment gave way, however, when I finally met the man. My mom had told me that my father was coming to see me, and that day was one of the happiest days of my young life. I was twelve years old at the time, and when he and I got together, I felt like I had known him all that time. Even at twelve, I could tell how alike we were. There was no doubt we belonged to each other.

I learned that my father didn't drink or smoke. His only vice, if you could call it that, was that he loved many different ladies. Later on, he did get it together, and had and raised my last four siblings with the woman I call my second mother, Barbara Nelson. I give her that title because 'stepmother' doesn't fit. The woman treated me like I'd come from her own womb and not from somebody else's.

Daniel Young, my maternal grandfather, was faithful to one woman, but he stumbled home to her every night. He had an issue with liquor. Lala never had to go get him from the arms of another woman, but he did have his liquor bottle. In spite of that, Popie was a successful and wealthy man.

He got it together, too. When I was five years old, a doctor came to the house and told Daniel Young that if he took one more drink, he would not live to see his next birthday–his liver was shot. Popie heeded the advice. He went cold-turkey sober from that day forward, and lived until he was eighty five years old.

My grandfather was a unique character, too. A Southern Gullah Geechee, he came from Sheldon, South Carolina. The Sea Islands were the landing place for the first African slave ships. Daniel Young was educated at the Penn School, a boarding school on St. Helena Island founded to teach the children of freed slaves. He distinguished himself there by playing on the Class of 1920 Penn School football team, and he's pictured with the rest of the team in a photo that now hangs in the Penn Center Museum.

My early judgment wasn't confined to my dad. True, he did have me and then wander off. However, my mother let him go. I wondered why my mother–or any woman, for that matter–would allow a man to do that, even though it happened all the time. That criticism went away because I found out later, when I was no longer a kid, that there was more to their story. From an adult perspective, I learned the truth in my own life of reaping what you sow–that judging something in another person can set you up to repeat the same behavior yourself.

I see that after having three daughters of my own–all with

the same woman. It's a mystery to me how we can judge other people—like I judged my father—and then as a father go through my own stuff. I think everybody has done this, had that moment of realizing, "Oh shoot, look at that!" My belief is that this is one way God gets our attention, like "Hey listen here, boy—watch this!" When He confronts you like that, all you can say is, "Oh my god, am *I* having issues, too?"

It also makes me see that while I was busy judging my mom and dad, I probably wasn't the best son I could've been back then. Now, when similar things go down with my own daughters, I think it goes to the way I treated my own parents. If they seem disrespectful, it feels like I'm getting my own disrespect back in my face. I could have been a much better son in thought, word and deed.

I judged my mom for having me out of wedlock. However, when my former wife and I had our first daughter, we weren't married, either. Make no mistake—the judgments we make always catch up with us. With me, I though I had gotten over some things and learned to forgive, and then here come my own kids. That's how it goes around. Maybe judgment is like poverty—something we can never get rid of.

Some of my early judgment of my mother and father came from comparisons I no doubt made between my real parents and my maternal grandparents, who ended up raising me mostly. In my grandparents' house on Maryton Road, I got to see how it was between married couples. When I went back and spent time with my mother, I saw the difference between that situation and a single-mother household. My mother did her best, but there was definitely more structure in Lala and Popie's home.

When I got to the age of starting my own family, I knew that what I wanted was what my grandparents had. Though we didn't start out that way, we got married after we had our first daughter, and then went on to have two more. Our first daughter was in our wedding. At that point, I had decided I wasn't putting my girls through what I'd gone through–living the first twelve years of my life wondering why my father didn't come around.

When he did come around after I'd been through the first twelve years of my life without him, he gave it to me straight. "Son," he began, "there's nothing we can do about this. I can't make up for lost time. And I'm not here to apologize. We can only go from here forward." It was a smart way to handle it, and I've always respected him for that. If he hadn't approached me that way, it would have been easy for me to backtalk and tell him, "Well, *you* didn't raise me–my *mamma* did." Somehow that morning in that house on Maryton Road, he and I managed to have a meeting of the minds. Garfenia McCrimmon had brought with him as much compassion as he could carry, and I took it as sincere.

From then on, I got to know him as I spent summers in

Detroit with him, my second mom and my other four siblings. My father was a Southern gentleman, and had come from Lumberton, North Carolina—another area in the costal plains of that state which became home for freed slaves and their descendants. His voice carried that soft Southern accent—not to the degree of a country bumpkin, but from the country to be sure.

Wherever he'd been in the time before I met up with him, after that meeting my father was always there for me. Even so, I was respectful of that fact. If I needed money for something, like later—for the semester of college, I never put it out there like he owed me something. I only called him up, told him what I needed. He'd talk it over with my second mother, and somehow they made a way for it to happen.

Our relationship took a different turn when, after he divorced my second mom, he was diagnosed with non-Hodgkin's lymphoma. Garfenia McCrimmon didn't think much of doctors or hospitals. I remember going out to Detroit when he was showing early signs of the disease. I'd spend the night with him in his apartment. The man couldn't sleep. He tossed and turned all night. Finally, I said, "Dad, come on. We're going to the doctor." The doctor found a lump on his neck, which had apparently been there for a long time. The diagnosis was made, but by then it was too late.

When you lose a parent, the temptation is to remember

the thing that took them, that illness or whatever. What I remember most about my father, however, was how very proud he was of me. Those summers I spent in Detroit made up for everything we'd missed out on in each other. He'd take me into stores with him. The ladies he knew there would nod toward me and ask, "Who's that?" Proudly, he would answer, "Oh, this is my *son*, Barry," in that smooth Southern drawl. "He's from *New Yawk, New Yawk*."

Looking at it all now, I can see how judgment, especially in families, can be a wicked, wicked thing. It's something that can haunt you from one generation to the next. Seems like when you finally get over the past generations and forgive their mistakes, along come your own children. If you're not wise to it, the cycle can start all over again and never end.

Life can surprise you, though, and things can come around full-circle in a positive light. I'm a two-time grandfather now. My oldest daughter Tachelle just gave me my second grandboy. Even before he was born, my prayer was, "Listen, God, a fine healthy grand*daughter* would be just fine. But after raising three girls, can you give me a break and send a little boy down here?"

I'm not sure if it was that prayer or maybe it was just meant to be, but Tachelle did give birth to a baby boy, Justin Emmanuel. I was ecstatic, and immediately began burning up Facebook with the news. The proud grandfather was letting it be known that he had a new grandboy, a fine addition to the Young McCrimmon line.

What I didn't know was how concerned my daughter was about little Justin Emmanuel. "Why are you putting this all up on Facebook?" she asked. She said some other things, too, and then hung up. I was confused. Why shouldn't we celebrate? Okay, I know the kid's got a long road ahead of him before he can leave the hospital. But THIS is the day the Lord has made. Aren't we supposed to rejoice and be glad in it? Can't we stop worrying about tomorrow for a minute and celebrate the birth of this little boy, and the miracle in that? (That was my thinking at the time. I now understand I should have put her feelings before my own.)

A lot of things were going on in my heart as I drove my Fiat down to Virginia to see the baby. I was still proud as I could be to have another grandson. But Tachelle was still on edge, and I didn't want any more of that. All I wanted was to love on my new grandson and leave the place in peace.

Sometime after that visit, I had a call from my youngest daughter, Dejia. Dejia knew that her sister had laid me out for the Facebook stuff. She began by explaining. "Daddy," she said, "Tachelle is just a little scared for the baby." They were feeding him intravenously, trying to work on his suction so he'd take a bottle. I didn't say anything (for once), but reflected on the fear that must be in every mother who just bore a child.

Luckily, Dejia wasn't done. "I just went to see Justin Emmanuel at the hospital," she told me. "He's getting bigger." I let that sink in. The child is growing. Things are going to be all right. Then Dejia said, "By the way, when I was about to leave, I leaned over Tachelle and the baby and said, "Honey, who does Justin look like? She said, "He looks like Daddy."

"You gotta be kidding me!" I blurted out. Here I was expecting Tachelle to say, "He doesn't look like Daddy." We finished talking and I hung up the phone. I remembered the fear I had when my first daughter was born. Tachelle was dealing with that same fear. Even though I didn't catch myself in a mirror, I know I was beaming. I start cheesing, dancing around the house all by myself. The boy is on his way. Tachelle and I may not be good yet, but we'll get there. And I got a new grandchild that looks just like me.

The Bible says that David danced privately before the Lord. You know me a little by now, and I do love to dance. At my retirement party, on a packed dance floor, I sweated out about ten gallons of water, and was lucky to have any soles left on my shoes by the end of the night. But sometimes the sweetest dance is the one we do is all by ourselves–the one that rejoices in this day, the one that's just between us and the One who gave us life.

LIVIN'
LOVE

RACE IS A SUBJECT that isn't often talked about with a lot of humor. I'm grateful then for one ticket-less rider on my train who taught me an important lesson about prejudice. In this chapter, I'll be using terms like black, white, African American and Caucasian—not as labels, but as a starting point for the discussion. In all honesty, I wear my thoughts about race on my sleeve. We will never get away from race, in my opinion. What's important is that we have the discussion. When we start having the discussion, we find out it's not as scary a subject as we think, and in some cases can even be funny.

In this case, it was a Caucasian man who boarded my

train at Grand Central. Shortly after we were moving, I began collecting tickets and learned that this man didn't have a ticket or money to buy one. I'm used to dealing with these situations as they come up fairly often. I always try to do it respectfully. "I'm sorry," I told the man, "but if you can't pay, you'll have to get off at 125th Street." That was the next stop.

I no sooner told him that than the man kicked up out of his seat, got down in the aisle between the seats flat on his face and began banging his head on the floor. "No, bro', please–*anywhere except 125th Street!*" The first thought that went through my mind was racial. Was this man saying he didn't want to get off at 125th Street–in the heart of Harlem–because he either didn't like or he feared black folks?" I was a little confused, too. Even if race was the issue here, there are many parts of Harlem where a white man might feel way more uncomfortable than on 125th Street. Not to mention that where I'd asked him to get out was on an elevated platform two stories above East 125th, so he wouldn't even be on the street level.

In this instance, it's easy to see the answer as 'racial' when we don't take time to think. The more I thought about it, however, as I watched this man banging his head in the aisle, it occurred to me that he might be autistic–which turned out to be the truth. Although this is the first time I'd dealt with him directly, he'd actually been riding on my train for years. Sometimes he'd be singing on the train, but this was the first time anyone could remember that he'd boarded without a means of paying.

I looked around at the other passengers, who were waiting to see how I would handle this. I wondered if they were judging him as I'd done first–thinking that this white 'racist' didn't want to be put off the train in a black neighborhood. I reached down and helped him up. "Listen, listen, bro'–" I said softly, "get up. Just have a seat over there, okay?" In that moment, the man taught me a lesson it would have taken a teacher a year or more to teach. This cat wasn't a racist; he was autistic, and that condition made him afraid. Not to say that people can't be racists, but not this time.

That was my first notable incident on the train where race could have become an issue. There were more to come. I remember the day a Latin guy called me a nigger. This story reminds me how much my regulars on the train had my back. The minute that guy said the n-word, two white guys on either side of him got up and were ready to take him out, beat him to the ground. I chose to let it go, and told the two guys, "No, it's okay," as I kept walking and those fellas sat down. Later, when I came back through, this Latin guy apologized to me. He said it under his breath, and I could smell that he'd been drinking.

There's a fundamental truth here–that when two people of different races argue, they will use the word that hurts the other person the most. Nigger. Cracker. Spic. We infer, when we hear a black man calling a white man "cracker" that he hates all white people. What I find is more often true is that when a black man calls a white man "cracker," it means he's really pissed of at the man and has picked the word he believes will inflict the most pain–and vice versa, of course.

One of two things is true–we're either all racists, or none of us are. It's all in how you judge it. I think of what happened to Paula Dean. Was she wrong to use the word "nigger"? I'll let you judge on that. What I have a problem with, however, is that she was punished by the press like she was the only white woman in the history of the world that had ever used the word. The media saw an opportunity to make her pay for the sins of other people who are truly racist. (What the media failed to report were how many people of color she employed who probably lost their jobs because of the whole thing.) They rode the story in a way that only perpetuates an ugly stereotype. To hell with it. I just ordered a set of Paula's kitchen utensils. The woman has suffered enough.

Another lesson I learned that helped, both onboard and off, is to use people's names. Whenever I'd go to the bank, I'd often be addressing a white person or black person behind the counter. I always looked at the name on their lapel pin, and I would use it. The expression on their face would change to a smile. That's my point: when we actually get to know each other, all that 'race' stuff changes up.

When you're open, race and even language stop being barriers. I learned how communicate with lots of people on the train that didn't speak English–Ecuadorians, Latvians, you name it. In thirty-three years, I got through the entire United Nations. All they needed to know was where their train was and what time it was leaving. I knew how to say that.

Now, I feel a little sorry for anybody who didn't have my job, because it opened me up to so many things. It gave me the opportunity to see that people are really people. They're great. They're a pain in the butt. And everything in-between. The more I saw that, the more tolerant I became. I had some beautiful times with everybody.

Because blacks and whites have historically been so insulated from each other, about the only time we'd interact was at work. As a conductor, I'd learned how to cross many color barriers. But when a coworker crossed that barrier one year by inviting me for Thanksgiving dinner, it was a powerful move I'll never forget.

Matt Mitchell was my engineer. Matt's white–part Irish, part Italian, and a buddy. I call him "my brother from another mother." He also knew my situation, that I was divorced and my kids were grown. We worked overtime on Thanksgiving Day. Near the end of our shift, Matt asked me, "Hey Slice, what are you doing after we get off work?"

I already had a plan, such as it was. Since the divorce, I'd spent a few holidays by myself and had kind of gotten used to it. "I'm getting some seafood, going home and getting my remote control in my hand and watching the game," I replied. Matt was short and to the point. "No, you're *not*," he informed me. "You're coming to my house for Thanksgiving."

It was a nice gesture, but something about knowing I'd be the only person of color there felt awkward. "No, I'm *not*," I told him. "I am not coming to your house for Thanksgiving." Matt wasn't giving up. "Oh yes, you *are*," he contradicted me. "Slice, you're coming to my house. My wife says to *get over here*."

"Oh boy, are you serious?" I asked. Matt nodded. "After work, follow me to my house," he said. That was it. We finished our shift, and I went to his house. As expected, I was the only African American there. Later, I wondered why I hesitated to go. Everyone there treated me wonderfully–his wife, his kids and his mother. Matt's my brother, and that's the bottom line. He'd insisted I come, and in the end I was glad I did. After all those years of working together, he really knew me. He made sure this was one Thanksgiving I wasn't going to spend alone in my living room with some seafood watching a Bowl game.

As my tolerance grew for the people who rode my train, I began more and more to see them as family. And as father who had raised three girls, it seemed natural for me to handle kids who were acting up. "Stop giving your mother a hard time," I'd say. My voice was stern, but I did it with a smile and mothers appreciated it. Sometimes it took a male voice to get those kids on point, and I did it across the board–to black kids, white kids and Latin kids. It was how my grandfather used to get us in line. He was a soft-spoken Geechee from the South who never had to raise his voice. But the pointed way he used to say, "Hey-hey-hey, boy..." made me obey him, no questions asked.

Once you've been a father, you begin to see that, in a way, black, white, brown, yellow or red, they're all our sons and daughters. I'll never forget a certain white gal on my train one day. Young gal–I assumed she went to Sarah Lawrence College because she boarded up in Bronxville. I'd walked by her a couple of times going up and down the car and could tell she was having the worst day. She was almost in tears.

Over time, I'd learned how to approach these things on the train. Folks are entitled to their privacy. In this case, however, the father in me said, "Talk to her." I sat down in the next seat, close enough speak with her, but not getting into her space. As a bald-headed, burly black man who is over six feet tall, I'd learned that my physical presence can be a little intimidating.

"I saw you were upset, and I don't know what you're going through," I began. "I only want you to know that whatever it is, things will get better. You can count on that." She looked at me, smiling for the first time since she got on the train.

Sometimes I think the biggest barrier to moving forward on the subject of race is we're not willing to admit where we're at with it. I developed a little test here, and if you choose to take it, I hope you will be brutally honest and not deceive yourself.

Barry's Sixty-Second Racial Tolerance Test
(*Please check the appropriate box*)
For Caucasian readers–
Q: Can you honestly say you have never used the word 'nigger'?
A: ❑ yes   ❑ no

Q: If you answered "no," did you use that word by mistake?
A: ❑ yes   ❑ no

For Readers of color–
Q: Can you honestly say you have never used the words 'cracker' or 'honkey'?
A: ❑ yes   ❑ no

Q: If you answered "no," did you use that word by mistake?
A: ❑ yes   ❑ no

I hope your honesty carried through both questions, because it's my point of view that when those words get used, it's no mistake. People use 'nigger,' 'spic,' 'cracker' and a host of other names because they want to inflict the most pain possible. Is it wrong? You're damned right it's wrong. But it's never a mistake.

Only when we admit our mistakes in regard to race do we open the way for change. And after all, isn't the name-calling part easy? We can change what comes out of our mouth, but changing what's in our hearts is a much bigger challenge. That's between us and God.

This week I saw that Philadelphia–the City of Brotherly Love–is formally apologizing to the widow of Jackie Robinson–the man who single-handedly broke the color barrier in major league baseball–for the blatantly racist way they treated Robinson when the Dodgers came to town to play the Phillies back in 1947. The entire team was turned away from their hotel because of the color of Jackie's skin–and that was just the start of it. I'm glad they're apologizing. But next time–for them and for all of us, let's not wait seventy years before we get to it.

(NOTE: *I was raised in Parkway Homes, a little enclave of a neighborhood in the hamlet of Greenburgh–a subset of the city of White Plains, New York. I thank "Lala" Helen Howcott-Young and "Popie" Daniel Young, my maternal grandparents, whose vision was much bigger than their bankroll. Lala masterminded a way to move on up. They carved out a place for me in their home and their hearts that blessed me in more ways than I can count.*

One of my favorite commuters on the train was one Mikey Epps, from my old neighborhood in Parkway Homes. I actually raised Mikey—meaning I was one of the big kids when he was coming up; Mikey was seven years my junior. He always beeped me to let me know he was on board. His message was short and simple: "The Sooooul Train," he'd write. It made me smile and even laugh out loud. Thank you, Mikey.

Our neighborhood was a unique place—a brotherhood, a sisterhood. Dedicating this to you all, the Parkway Homes Nation, with a massive amount of love. B.D.Y.)

I GOT THE
MUSIC IN ME

BECAUSE OF MUSIC, our world is becoming one. Look around. If you go to the live performance of a black artist, you'll see a lot of white people in the audience. Or go to a concert by a white artist or group and what do you see? Lots of white people, yes—but also a number of black people, too.

When I was coming up, that wasn't the way. If you were African American and listened to Led Zeppelin, KISS or AC/DC in our neighborhood, you'd get asked, "Why're you listening to 'white-boy' music?" However, things switched up for me when I spent summers with my father in Detroit. Out there, all my friends were guitar players, and they listened to the likes of

KISS, AC/DC and Fleetwood Mac. I handed them the same line they would have handed me back in Greenburgh: "Why are you listening to all that white-boy music?!"

It wasn't long, however, before I was listening to Stevie Nicks, too. I'm so thankful now for my boys back in Detroit, because today I listen to everything. I'll never give up my soul, R&B and funk, but I also found a love for the music of David Bowie, Elton John and many, many others. From then on, music has never had a color for me, and I know it never will. Music is my all-time favorite thing in life. This may sound like a proverb, but I'd take a bad tune to an argumentative woman any day of the week.

It is my firm belief that music can be life-altering. It has changed the way I see the world. It has changed the way I judge people and situations. It has transported me to places I would never have reached without it. What follows here are my own personal liner notes to this compilation CD of my life-altering tracks. Depending on when you came up, some may be familiar. Others you may not know, but will definitely want to check out.

Barry's Playlist of Life-Altering Songs:

1. Seals & Crofts. *Summer Breeze*. Summer Breeze. Warner Bros. 1972. LP.

There are two notable version of this song, one by Seals and Crofts and then a slower version by the Isley Brothers. I can't hear this song without thinking of Carol Rogers, a high school friend of my mother's. They both came from big families. Miss Rogers passed away suddenly around the summer of 1972, when this song was released. She had five children: Barry, Everett–who was my best friend, Renee, Kendall and Wanda. I always feel sad when I hear that song, thinking of Miss Carol who passed away way too soon. She was also considered hands-down the prettiest mom in all of Greenburgh.

2. Son Little. *About A Flood*. Son Little. ANTI-, 2014. LP.
I love this song because it's so smooth and melodic. The song asks, "What are we going to do about it?" Like a lot of things in life, we have to ask, "What *are* we going to do if there's a flood?"– or if we break up or if someone passes away. We learn to adjust. I feel like this is a song of surrender. If we can learn to let go whenever that "What if… ?" hits us, we can find peace.

3. Lauryn Hill. *I Get Out* (Live). MTV Unplugged No. 2.0. Columbia, 2002. CD.
The message in this song–getting out of whatever box people have put you it–helped me through the lowest point in my life. I had become so disillusioned by the judgment of a group of 'be-

lievers' I was part of at that time. I would listen to *I Get Out* over and over, often with tears running down my face. It freed me, because through it I realized that my 'belief' was between me and God—*how* I worship, *when* I worship and *where* I worship Him is a thing that exists between me and Him and nobody else. Hill recorded this album when she had freed herself from the box she'd been in—a band that waited around for her to write another song they could make money from. She realized she didn't need them and fired them. She picked up her guitar, walked out and recorded the album, MTV Unplugged.

4. Lauryn Hill. *I Gotta Find Peace of Mind* (Live). MTV Unplugged No. 2.0. Columbia, 2002. CD.

Another powerful song (and I recommend this whole album) where Hill talks about feeling like she's going crazy, which was the same feeling I had at the time but couldn't express it myself. She actually breaks down by the end of the song, but it was also a breakthrough, as she began to believe in words like "possible" and "haveable" and "tangible." What's impossible becomes possible. Those words opened the door to the prison her mind had become and, in that act of liberation, she (and I) found peace.

5. Ohio Players. *Fire*. Fire. Mercury, 1974. LP.

This song is my signature. I love to dance to it. It makes no differ-

~ *continued on page 77* ~

A YOUNG FAMILY CHRISTMAS – *Front row, left to right*: Barbara Young (Aunt Bobby), Carolyn Young (Auntie Cubs), Patricia Young (Aunt Patty); *Middle row*: Sue T. Young (my mother), Helen Howcott Young ("Lala," my grandmother), Theodore D. Young (Uncle Teddy), Eloise L. Young (Aunt Weezie), Chuck Young (Uncle Chucky); *Standing, far left*: Daniel H. Young ("Popie," my grandfather).

MY MOM – My beautiful mom, Sue Theola Young holding a very young Barry. A pacifier was the only way to keep me quiet–then and now.

PARENTS TOGETHER – Sue Theola Young and Garfenia McCrimmon came together to help me celebrate my wedding on December 15, 1985. I treasure this photo, because it's the first picture I had of both my parents together.

FAMOUS DRIVE-BY – My cameo appearance in rap artist Shinehead's 1988 music video, "Chain Gang." I happened to be in the right place at the right time, and the crew that was shooting the video recruited me for my few seconds of fame. My flashing that peace sign was spontaneous and unplanned.

ALL ABOARD! – This random shot was taken one year before my retirement by a photographer practicing with his camera.

LOST & FOUND – My big brother, Seth Vanderberg (*right*), one of my thirteen siblings I recently reconnected with.

THREE VERY IMPORTANT LADIES in my life: My oldest daughter, Tachelle Dene (Young) Craddock (*above*); My second oldest, Lacquelle Jene Young (*lower left*); My youngest, Dejia Janelle Loise Biney (*lower right*).

LIKE POP-POP – (*above*) Getting fly for Auntie Dejia's 2015 wedding with my first grandson, Cairo Bleu. Sharp as tacks in our matching shirts and ties.

PASSING THE HAT (*right*) Handing down my conductor's hat to my grandson Cairo during my retirement blowout bash in November of 2015. Not sure he understood the significance, but it will hit him in about thirty years, when it's his turn to pass the hat on.

THE MATRIARCH AND ME – My dear Aunt Weezie and I wearing our best blues in Atlanta during a weekend legacy conference celebrating her 50+ years in the ministry.

PROUD PAPA & GRANDPAPA – Celebrating my grandson Justin Emmanuel's baptism with my three daughters: Lacquelle (*left*), Tachelle (*center, with Justin Emmanuel*), and Dejia (*right*).

PHANTOM CONDUCTOR – My regulars wish me a happy retirement as I arrived on the platform at Grand Central Terminal after my final run. I dressed for the occasion. My last day happened to fall on the day before Halloween.

Dear Barry,
Thank you for giving me the J train, the J train shirt, and the Christmas ornament! I like them very much!
♡
Julian

Left – Showing my moves on the top deck of the Carnival Splendor cruise ship. Right – A treasured drawing given to me by Julian, one of my favorite young passengers. This kid was a constant joy, the highlight of my tedious night shifts.

DRESSED FOR RETIREMENT – Trying to be dapper for my retirement bash, November 2015. I have a thing for good hats, as did my grandfather, Daniel "Popie" Young. I call this my OG style–Original Gentleman. I stand here as the proud product of four families: Youngs, McCrimmons, Howcotts and McCoys.

November 16, 2015

Mr. Mac King
WNYW Fox 5 News
205 E 67th St
New York, NY 10021

Dear Mac:

Thank you so much for the Fox 5 News feature you did
on my retirement from the Metro North Railroad. It was
a great piece, and I'm humbled by the thought that what
was a big milestone for me was also newsworthy to you
and your VIewers.

This month, I will begin writing a book about my 33 years
on the railroad. I'd love to send you a copy when the book
is published, sometime after the middle of next year.

Thanks again for the great feature. You helped me ride
out in style.

Best regards,

Barry D. Young
Metro North Railroad Conductor, *retired*

February 18, 2004

ERIC B. KAVIAR
ATTORNEY
712 THIRD AVENUE
BROOKLYN, NEW YORK 11232
TEL. (718) 965-6146
FAX (718) 768-5077

Peter A Cannito, President
Metro North Railroad
The Metropolitan Transportation Authority
347 Madison Avenue
New York, New York 10017

Re: Wallet Return, Train 571, 2/17/04
     Thank you

Dear President Cannito:

I am a regular commuter on Metro North living in Hartsdale.

Last night my wife met me at Grand Central Station using
Metro North in order to have a dinner with mends. Unfortu-
nately she lost her wallet on the train coming into Manhattan.
The train she was on departed Hartsdale Station at approximately 5:00 P. M. While still in Grand Central station we
realized that her wallet was missing. We went to the District
5 Police Station at Grand Central Station and reported the
incident. The officer at the desk was very professional and most
helpful in taking our information regarding this loss. This officer immediately contacted persons at the train she had been
on to determine if they could find the wallet. At that point we
thought the wallet would not be recovered; however, we provided our information to the officer. We then met our friends,
had a pleasant dinner and returned home by Metro North.

When we returned home at approximately 11 :30 P. M. we were pleasantly surprised, I should say shocked that there was a message from one of your supervisors, Donald Clifford. Mr. Clifford left his telephone number with the message that the wallet had been recovered and it appears that all its contents were in place. We immediately called Mr. Clifford who provided us with directions to the North White Plains train station in order that we may retrieve the wallet.

When we arrived at the North White Plains train station around midnight we met Mr. Clifford and another gentleman who were most professional and polite and returned the wallet to my wife. As Mr. Clifford thought, all of my wife's contents were in the wallet including various credit cards, cash and personal items. To say we were surprised is an understatement. My wife wanted to give a money reward to the gentleman who retrieved the wallet; however, Mr. Clifford stated that that would be against MTA policy and refused to accept my wife's persistent attempts to reward the gentleman who turned in her wallet. I then asked Mr. Clifford for the name of the gentleman who retrieved the wallet in order that I could write a letter of his alertness, conscientiousness and honesty in order that his supervisor is aware of his fine actions. The gentleman who found and returned my wife's valuables is Conductor Barry Young.

You should be proud and honored to have such fine people working for the MTA. Again, many thanks.

Sincerely yours,
Eric B. Kaviar

"THE LETTER"
"You People" a letter to my commuter and Passengers

"You people" have been my lifeline for 33 years & 3 months. Normally the words "You People" carries a negative, stereotypical connotation with it, but not here!

Literally you people bought excitement, laughter & simply crazy fun into my life.

As your Conductor, I honestly enjoyed and looked forward to coming to work each and everyday. Many of you have asked why I was always so upbeat. Well truly can say 98% of it was because of "you people". You gave me a whole lot to smile about. You gave me the ride of a lifetime. We really had a BALL. I'm seriously not sure how I would have made it. Through some of my life stressors, had it not been for "You People" and your smiling faces. I want to especially THANK SCRUFFY TIGER, SLUGGER, SCOOTER, COOPER, ANGEL, EBONY, GOLDI-LOCKS, BUTTERCUP AND PRINCESS TOO! (Oh and I could never forget Mr. & Mrs. !). Long story short 8 years or so ago, I went through a "separation of sorts" which in turn caused me not to wanna really get up out of bed to even come to work. I then remember praying my daily prayer in which I asked God to just give me the extra strength I needed to get from the house to the train aisle .. ie. MY STAGE. He did that and then "you people" did what you do ... everyday. YOU LIFTED ME, YOU LIFTED MY SPIRITS when I really just wanted to fall down & fall out. I made through those most difficult days thanks to "you people"! Days, weeks, months, and even years 'You people' did that for me! Unknowingly you lifted me out of the doldrums. I will always love and appreciate you all for that. When you smiled, greeted and joked with me I was able to reciprocate and the coolest part of it all was it actually made US FAMILY. Oh don't get it twisted you are and always will be my TRAIN FAMILY. You made it all so bearable for me. I was even able to learn things about myself,that previously I had no idea of. I'd love to say THANK YOU to each and Everyone of you all. Spiritually I'm taking each of you with me wherever I go. I ask that you do the same, with much Love.

Your Conductor 4 life
PS As I say I love you, of course is so not physical. The love I have for you started in my mind, THEN GREW IN MY HEART

~ *continued from page 64* ~

ence if I have a partner or I'm home alone. If I'm in a *store* and I hear *Fire*, I'm dancing.

6. Nat Townsley, Jr. *What Does It All Mean.* I Fell in Love With God. ABC, 1975. LP.

When I was in high school, we had these Young/Howcott family reunions every year at Mohansic Park in Yorktown Heights, NY. We had the best spot in the park for these reunions, just around a bend where you could see everybody arrive and shout out, "Hey, there's 'Cuda (my nickname at the time, short for "barracuda") because they identified our little Chevette. Everybody would get announced by the people who were already there. We had a set of cousins, my grandmother's sister's children. One cousin was named Darren Diamond. Darren had three brothers from down in the Central Islip/Amityville area. Darren was cute, and all the girls had a cousin crush on him. One year Darren and his friends 'borrowed' a motorcycle. Darren gave up his helmet to his friend riding with him. Darren was killed on that motorcycle by a hit-and-run driver; the friend he gave his helmet to survived. I remember going to Darren's funeral, and the struggle with my grandmother over it, because Lala was strict and didn't want me to miss a day of school. It was the saddest thing. Those little girls were falling over his casket so much at the wake that Darren's mother had to close it for the funeral. I used to listen to this gospel album my Aunt Weezie had at the Marytown Road house by Rev. Nat Townsley, Jr. from Brooklyn. I listened to his *What Does It All Mean* over and over, crying and asking, "Okay God, are you trying to tell me I'm never going to see my cousin Darren again?" At that age, I really didn't understand death–especially the death of somebody my age, because Darren was such lively, crazy and fun cousin to hang out with at those family reunions. It was inconceivable. In my mind, my cousin Darren was too young to die. To this day, that song still reminds me of asking God a pretty fundamental question, "What does it all mean?"

7. The Beatles. *Don't Let Me Down*. Let It Be. Apple, 1970. LP. Strictly the best band in the world, in my opinion, hired the best and most prolific organist to play with them on this very special track. I'd loved this song for years without knowing that it was Billy Preston playing the organ. I posted a comment about it on Facebook, and one of my best friends, Darryll Leak, clued me in that it was Billy Preston playing. I'm still shocked that I never knew that. I had to go back and look at the video twice. This was in the days before Preston blew out his Afro; he has a small one back then. It was the Beatles last live performance together on the cold and windy rooftop of Apple Records office building in London. Preston also contributed a memorable organ solo in the song *Get Back*. He's the only musician besides the Beatles themselves ever to be credited on one of their albums, earning Billy Preston the honorary title of "The Fifth Beatle."

8. **Eric Roberson.** *Anymore.* B-Sides, Features & Heartaches. Dome, 2014. CD.

This song has been particularly relevant to me in the last couple of years. It talks about relationships, and what happens when they don't work any more, and the feeling of loving someone when that love is not "reciprocated"–which can be funny and make you angry at the same time. I've seen Eric Roberson perform a couple of times, and even have a picture of us together when he played at S.O.B.'s in Manhattan. The first time I saw him live, I bought his album from his father, who was selling his son's CDs in the back of the jazz place where he was performing.

{B-Side Note: When my Internet radio station is up and running, I will be playing Eric Roberson. My beef with black radio (and I'll keep it brief here, but more is to come) is they only play mega-hit artists who are payola for the station. They'll play songs that have little girls moving their midsections around and singing about 'coco' (aka 'cocaine') without even knowing what's coming out of their mouths, but they won't play any new black artists–Raheem DeVaughn, Alice Smith, Eric Roberson, Leon Bridges, Son Little and the like, something I intend to correct when I am live and on the air.}

9. Alabama Shakes. *Don't Wanna Fight*. Sound & Color. ATO, 2015. CD.

This is another song that echoes my relationship experience. Like, "We've argued about this, we've had misunderstandings about the same subject *ten times*. How 'bout this? I don't wanna fight no more."

10. Raheem DeVaughn. *Mister Right*. So Radio. Aries, 2007. CD.

Even though I have a few quirks, I like to think of myself as Mr. Right. When I'm trying to impress a lady, I would think of this song and say to her, "Yeah, I've made some mistakes but I'm a grown man now, and I think I'm the right one for you (lol)."

11. Luther Vandross. *Never Too Much*. Never Too Much. Epic, 1981. CD.

After I graduated from high school and when I was about twenty one, I fell in love with this girl but was afraid to tell her. She came along about the time the song came out, when I was actually in my shy stage. This girl was so petite and so pretty that to this day, I swear I'm still in love with her. *Never Too Much* was our song. I know it by heart, and can still recite it word for word. Again, it feels like I wrote this song with my life experience, because part of the song talks about not knowing what to say or how to touch her and that's exactly the way it was between us.

12. **Black Coffee.** *Superman (feat. Bucie).* Home Brewed. Jellybean Soul, 2009. MP3.

A new song I found last year. New, that is, until all my house-head and club-head friends told me, "Barry, that's *old.* That's *been* out." I like the way the song starts as a house/club mix, but after the first twenty seconds, it turns into a freaking love song. In the video, the way she walks out through that club takes me into another world. She sings, "Can you be my Superman?" As a single man, at times I'm wondering, "Can I improve myself to where some woman would say to me, "Can you be my Superman?"

My daughter called me that one time. I drove her to Pittsburgh to school–seven hours straight, then I turned right around and drove straight back to New York. When I called her, she said, "Daddy, you can *not* be home." I said, "Yeah, I am. I have to go to work tomorrow." She said, "Oh my god, Daddy–you are my Superman." Having spent my days as a player, I'm at that point in my life where it isn't about a lot of women. It's about that one special woman who will call me her Superman.

13. **Fleetwood Mac.** *Dreams.* Rumours. Warner Bros., 1977. LP.

When this song came out, I was going through a transformation. Prior to its release, I primarily listened to soul and funk. Even though it's not a 'rock' song, *Dreams* opened me up. This is an extension of what I said earlier about summers spent with my father in Detroit. I came in from New York with this Afrocentric music agenda to encounter a group of black kids my age who were not only listening to KISS, AC/DC and Fleetwood Mac, but also learning how to play this music on their guitars. I'd been judging everything by what I perceived as 'white' music or 'black' music until I started really listening to these other 'white boy' groups. I came back to New York after those summers with all these albums. My friends generously gave them up because they could see I couldn't live without this music. The more I listened, the more I could hear what they were hearing. Back home, however, my New York crew let me have it for about a year. "What are you listening to?!" they asked. I had to man up and say, "Hey, I *like* KISS." And that was it. Once you get a taste of something, you can't help it. You like what you like. I was like, "Forget this 'color' stuff." That's when music ceased to exist for me behind racial divides.

14. **Edie Brickell.** *What I Am.* Shooting Rubberbands at the Stars. Geffen, 1988. CD.
My friends have said to me, "You know, you're ahead of your time. How did you know that *What I Am* by Edie Brickell would be sampled by Grand Puba and the Brand Nubian in a rap song? I always loved *What I Am* because of the bass line. Three years lat-

er, Brand Nubian (one of Westchester's own) with Gran Puba–their head rapper and a guy I know personally–took Brikell's music and made a song called *Slow Down,* which is beautiful. It is Edie Brickell and the New Bohemians' old beat. Edie is married to Paul Simon. There's a great message about judgment in the song, which says *I am what I am* and *you are what you are,* so let's be cool with that and not judge each other. We are who we are.

15. **Citizen Cope.** *107 Degrees.* The Lincoln Lawyer (Soundtrack). Lakeshore, 2011. MP3.

Clarence Greenwood (aka "Citizen Cope") is one of the most soulful Caucasian men I've ever heard play a guitar. He's also in a relationship with African American singer and songwriter Alice Smith. The two have never recorded *107 Degrees* together, but you can see them doing a duet version of this song on You Tube. I was lucky enough to hear them at a live concert at the Tarrytown Music Hall. I'd heard the song before, because it's on Citizen Cope's album. But this duet version takes it to a whole other level. She hit this one note and it was like the room came to a complete standstill.

16. **James Brown.** *Say It Loud.* Say It Loud - I'm Black and I'm Proud. Vox, 1968. LP.

Brown wrote this song the year Dr. Martin Luther King was shot.

It is quintessential funk. I remember my mother listening to *Say It Loud*, even though she was really more into The Supremes, The Four Tops and The Temptations. This song came out toward the end of the Civil Rights Movement. For me personally, it was very empowering, especially when Brown sings about dying on his feet versus living on his knees. I was young at the time and I know Brown intended these lyrics for a more adult audience, but even as a kid I got what he was saying. At the time, every boy my age had Afro socks–"African Liberation Socks," we called them. If you're not familiar with them, these were white cotton sweat socks we pulled up to our knees striped with the African liberation colors–red, black and green. This song has a powerful beat and I love to dance to it, but it also empowered black people to think more of themselves during that time.

17. **Jeff Tweedy.** *Low Key*. Sukierae. Anti/Epitaph, 2014. MP3. This is a song I never even thought I would want to listen to. I try to be open-minded, though, and found out that I really love *Low Key*. It's a very cool what I call "white-boy" song–and by now you'll know I'm not saying that in a negative way at all. Tweedy used to be with Wilco, the alternative rock band out of Chicago. This song always makes me think of my former wife, who was low key–pretty much kept it cool and didn't get overly excited about things. Listen to it and you'll also hear how much this dude was

inspired by The Beatles.

18. Aerosmith. *Walk This Way.* Toys in the Attic. Columbia, 1975. LP.

I always liked this song for the heavy guitar riffing, and liked it even more when Run-D.M.C. rapped this song. There's a great moment in the music video where Aerosmith's very own Steven Tyler uses his mike stand to bash a hole in the wall and sticks his head through that hole into the room where Run-D.M.C. is rapping *Walk This Way.* I love the whole thing because it makes my point about music having no color, that two groups of artists from two totally different genres of music can come together on the same song. To me, Aerosmith and Run-D.M.C. is one of the coolest mash-ups ever.

19. Elton John. *Benny and the Jets.* Goodbye Yellow Brick Road. MCA, 1974. LP. One of my all-time favorite tracks. I don't know if that's because of the piano chops, or Elton's voice, or that unforgettable beat. I can play this one any time.

20. Funkadelic. *Maggot Brain.* Maggot Brain. Westbound, 1971. LP.

This instrumental piece is a must-listen for anyone aspiring to play lead guitar. George Clinton was the force behind both the

Parliament and Funkadelic bands and has a phenomenal discography. I used to go hear these guys at Madison Square Garden with my boys back in the day. Unbelievable stuff. You Tube it and you'll see what I mean.

21. Funkadelic. *Groove Allegiance.* One Nation Under a Groove. Warner Bros., 1978. LP.
This song's lyrics are a riff on the Pledge of Allegiance we all said in school. It keeps moving to different levels, never settling on the same beat. It's a beautiful song. You have to listen to it.

22. Funkadelic. *Cholly.* One Nation Under a Groove. Warner Bros., 1978. LP.
"I was strung out on Bach and Beethoven was my thing..." is how this song starts out. The words will bug you out, because it's so funny the things they put together in this funkadelic acid format. This is a great example of when the right words get together with the right beat. The sum becomes exponentially better than the parts.

23. David Bowie. *Fame.* Young Americans. RCA, 1975. LP.
Another one of my all-time favorites. Funky space odyssey. I remember *Fame* as one of the first songs by a Caucasian artist that they played at my dance parties. We had these mostly African

American hip hop dance parties, and when that song came up, nobody cared whether the singer was black or white. We danced to it—and boy, did we dance. Nothing else needs to be said. Listen to it.

24. **Led Zeppelin.** *Kashmir.* Physical Graffiti. Swan Song, 1975. LP.
Absolutely love this song. The bass takes over the place.

25. **Bootsy Collins.** *Pinocchio Theory.* Single. Warner Bros., 1975. LP.
Bootsy Collins is under the George Collins Parliament-Funkadelic umbrella. According to Bootsy, if you 'fake' the funk, your nose will grow. That's the 'Pinocchio Theory.' This song always takes me back to the summers I spent in Detroit with my father. My friends and I would ride around with the car windows open and blasting this song.

26. **Mazzy Star.** *Fade Into You.* So Tonight That I Might See. Capitol, 1975. CD.
Another must-listen-to. A hauntingly, heavenly delightful song.

27. **Jack Garratt.** *Worry.* Phase. Interscope, 2016. CD.
I think about the meaning of this song, which I believe is "Don't

worry." So maybe he should have called it *Don't Worry*. Another underplayed artist, in my opinion. I play this song for a lot of friends and they've all said, "Who *is* that?" They've never heard of him. Then they all want to buy it.

28. **House of Pain.** *Jump Around.* House of Pain. Tommy Boy, 1992. CD.

Everlast is an American rapper who was also part of the hip-hop group La Coka Nostra. What I like about this song is that Everlast presents Irish culture as he's singing and rapping, including the St. Patrick's Day Parade. He uses bagpipes as a major source for the music in this song. Those bagpipes are playing a single note throughout, but the way he mixes it shows you what a master he is. Everlast is an amazingly versatile artist. He picked up an acoustic guitar in 2013 and recorded an album called *The Life Acoustic*. I can't wait to see what this dude will do next.

CALLED MY
OLD NICKNAME

JOBS GET MONOTONOUS. Even as much as I enjoyed being a conductor, you do the same thing every day, over and over. You walk the aisles. You take tickets. You make announcements. I discovered, however, when I started using nicknames, the ride became more like a party–both for my passenger and for me.

Nicknames had been a part of my life from a young age. They called my mother 'Wick' because she was so slim. Mother's twin brother, Uncle Teddy, was the source of many of our family nicknames. My aunt, Carolyn Cook Young, was called 'Auntie Cubs' because she was the baby cub of the family, the youngest among her seven siblings.

When I started using nicknames for my passengers,

I stayed respectful. Before anything came out of my mouth, I would gauge how it might land on them. I never wanted it to seem mean-spirited; that wasn't the point. The point was to engage them in a fun way that made them forget the monotony of their commute and allow them to feel relaxed and at home on my train.

I had a list of nicknames that seemed to work well on women of color:

Ebony	Queen
Ebony Princess	Queenie
Ebony Pearl	Honey
Merlot	Penny
Cinnamon	Angel
Mocha	Angelica
Olivia	Cocoa Puff
Buttercup	Princess

I'd use 'Cocoa Puff' on younger girls who had their hair done in a pair of Afro puffs, like my sister April had when she was little. Girls loved that one. I'd take their ticket and say, "Thank you, Cocoa Puff" and it would always bring a smile to their face.

There were others, like 'Sassy, but Classy.' I used to use that on one classy-looking African American woman who got off at the Fleetwood stop every day. She told me she went to a Baptist Church in Mount Vernon. I'd address her by saying, "Excuse me, Sassy but Classy." She'd keep walking away from me, but that nickname always got a laugh out of her and she left my train with a big smile on her face.

Passengers got attached to their nicknames. One of my regulars, a Pakistani lady, loved to be called 'Princess.' When I forgot to use her 'royal' title, she was quick to remind me. "Hey Barry, I didn't get my nickname today." Not only that, she wanted an exclusive on it. "I'm the only 'princess' here," she'd tell me firmly. "Don't you dare use that name on anyone else."

Sometimes the nicknames were born out of situations. I had one lady that rode my train into Grand Central Terminal. When she got seated, she would often pull her hat down over her nose and catch a little sleep. Her nickname became 'The Mad Hatter.' When the train arrived and she put her hat up, I'd say, "Good Morning, Mad Hatter." I always got a laugh in return.

My list of men's nicknames was more extensive:

Scrappy	Ferocious
Tiger	OG
Ace	Tchaikovsky
Speed Racer	Beethoven
Slim	Bach
Munch 'n Crunch	Brahams
Ice	Professor

Dice

Smokey

Slice

Slappy

Black

Rock

Vanilla Slice

Rocky

Junior

Commodore

Captain Crunch

Commander

Smiley

Admiral

Happy

General

Champ

Dictator

Slugger

Scooby

Scruffy

Snappy

Skipper

Red

Sparky

Blue

Slippery

Doctor

Loud & Out Proud

Chocolate Mini

Corporal

Ralph Cramden

Mighty Mouse

Ed Norton

Brown

Prince

Sonny

King

Scooter

Clark Kent

Captain

Spunky

Cooper

Klondike

Mac

Lefty

Jack

Columbo

Zack	Esquire
Butter	Spanky
Ducky	Perry Mason
Fearless	Tex

Some of these might make you wonder how I got away with it. Call the wrong guy 'Spanky' and you might wind up with his fist in your face. I always thought it through before I nicknamed anyone, and if I found out by reaction that they didn't like that particular nickname or being nicknamed in general, I let that be the end of it.

I also had a special routine for people sitting side-by-side in one of the train's two-seaters. "Thank you, Jack and Jill..." I would say if they looked like a married couple. They died laughing. There were others, too, for these 'couples': Samson and Delilah, Mary and Joseph, and Ken and Barbie.

My all-time favorite, though, for a man and woman sitting together in those two-seaters was "Mister and Missus." As I punched their tickets, I'd confidently say, "Thank you, Mister and Misses"– and watch what would happen next. If they were strangers to each other, the woman would look over at her perceived 'husband' and sometimes cringe at the thought. On the other hand, the man would sometimes look over at the lady and, if she was attractive and to his liking, he would smile, considering the possibility. I wasn't trying to be a matchmaker, but I now wonder if I had started anything, if any of those strangers ever actually became Mister and Missus.

I want to also say a word about 'Loud and Out Proud.' I have a brother who is gay whom I love very much. Therefore, I have a lot of respect for the LGBT community, because I know they are constantly being judged by straight people, church people, you name it. "Thank you, Loud and Out Proud" was a way for me to acknowledge passengers who I knew were part of that community. I chose carefully when to use this nickname, also considering who else might be in earshot. It got me a smile, time after time–a smile that said back, "Thanks for not judging me. Thanks for the respect."

You could argue that all these nicknames slowed down business. If I had simply said, "Tickets, please" the process would have moved along efficiently, probably more efficiently that it did with the inclusion of 'buddy' or 'cinnamon' or 'sassy but classy.' The transaction is quicker, but I figured that was a pretty monotonous way to live. However, when you call somebody by name–either their real name or one of my nicknames, a light comes into their eyes. Now they're looking you, actually making eye contact. The ride that had felt impersonal now was warmer and more friendly–for them and for me.

The more passengers I got to know in this way, the larger

my world became. The nicknames had become something fun for all of us. I never expected to get anything in return for connecting with my passengers; it just sort of happened. People offered me tickets to sporting events. They gave me their business cards, promising to help me out if I needed their professional service. After one incident with a passenger, I had a guy stand up, give me his card and say, "Hey, I'm an attorney. If you get any flack over this, give me a call–I saw the whole thing."

As the nicknames went out, the whole thing came back to me like a boomerang. They called me by name, or called me 'Slice,' which was my own nickname. As they saw I supported them, they were supportive of me. I could tell when somebody was having a bad day. My *Hang in there, bro...* went a long way. And when I was going through my little divorce, they had the same encouraging words for me.

In a way, we had become doctors for each other. I bucked them up, and when I needed the same, they gave it to me. Today I realize how much that mattered. Now, we were somehow together in all of this, thanks to a few corny nicknames and a lot of goodwill on both ends.

The whole nickname thing almost came to an end, however, from one passenger complaint. One evening I was told by the train master that a woman had complained, having heard me refer to two passengers as 'Frick and Frack.' Things often sound bad outside their original context. I know that I hadn't said it in a mean-spirited way; that's not my nature. But officially, I was told it was inappropriate and unprofessional and that I had to cool it.

I felt hurt and angry. How could this routine that everybody loved be taken away by the negative comment of one woman? What ever happened to the will of the majority? Still, I respected the reprimand and cut out the nicknames. The commute was back to being dull and monotonous, for the passengers and for me. As I walked up and down the aisles, people would ask, "*Hey, Barry, where's my nickname?!*" They looked disappointed. I shrugged. They weren't half as disappointed as I was.

One of my regulars, a guy from Bronxville, asked me point-blank what had happened. He filed a counter-complaint with my superiors. (Bloom is a great guy with a mischievous sense of humor. He once gave me a list of nicknames he thought were well-suited for using on him, including 'Beetle Nose' and 'Pencil Dick.' Of course I never called him any of that, but his list still makes me laugh out loud). Here's the letter he wrote:

September 23, 2013

To Whom It May Concern:

Within the past few weeks, I noticed that my (and everyone else's) favorite conductor, Barry D. Young has ceased his always-enjoyable routine of thanking all of his passengers with his perennial set of delightful nicknames.

Tonight I asked him what was going on, and he informed me that one person had taken offense to being called something utterly harmless, and he had been written up as unprofessional.

You must be kidding.

Barry is the MOST professional conductor I've had the pleasure of riding with. He not only does his job perfectly, but always manages to put everyone on the train in a good mood with his routine. It is clear that he loves his job—and it is always a nice treat to see someone who does.

I've been riding with him for three years, and he has never called anyone anything the least bit offensive. Some of his favorites: Thank you, Champ! Thank you, Junior! Thank you, Spike! Thank you, Mister and Missus! (regardless if whether they know each other), Thank you, Frick and Frack! (two Swiss skaters from the 1930s), Thank you, Slugger! Yeah, *really awful stuff.*

Whatever mindless bureaucrat made the decision to silence Barry has made commuting a lot less pleasurable.

This is just plain wrong, and I am determined to fix it. Here's how:

1. By nature of my profession, I have extensive and personal access to all local news outlets. When they get hold of this, you will look like idiots.

2. I hope you enjoy this letter, because you'll be getting one every week until I get my nickname back.

It is rare to find someone that can bring a little joy to so many people. For you to treat him like a pariah is both stupid and wrong.

Regards,

Dr. Jonathan Bloom

PS– Please feel free to invite the person who complained to kiss my Jewish ass. Now *that* is unprofessional. Go ahead. Write me up.

Something happened after that letter hit the front office.

I never knew if they feared getting weekly letters from this out-spoken passenger, or they took him seriously about calling in the press. Whatever it was, before too long the nicknames were back. Once more, I started punching tickets and expressing my grati-tude with a courteous "Thank you, Cocoa Puff." Somehow we'd made it over the thin ice, and now we were all back to smooth skating, with special thanks to Frick and Frack. Oh, and "Thank *you*, Mister and Missus."

DANCING WITH
MYSELF

IN JOHN'S GOSPEL, there's a story about Jesus finding his disciples by the sea after they'd been fishing all night. When Jesus asks them if they'd had any luck, they tell him they hadn't caught a single fish. I think about that story as a single man now, back in the dating swim and wondering on which side of the boat to cast my net.

You make a lot of judgments in relationships, and especially in romantic ones. I don't want to be unfairly judged myself, but I've observed that I don't always give others the slack I'd like to get myself. For instance, if I'm talking to a young lady and I notice her language is foul, I tend to think, "Whoa, wait a minute..." and judge her based on that. Then I'll get judged in a certain way by a lady just because I'm a very friendly and outgoing guy, and my intentions toward her are gentlemanly. The Apostle Paul was right. The thing we don't want to do is what we usually end up doing.

Guys my age soon discover that the current dating world is much different than the one I left to get married XX years ago. I warn you in advance that some of this talk may seem old-fashioned, but I'm an old school guy, so you get what you get. Back in the day, people were polite. If I walked all the way across the dance floor to ask a woman to dance, she wouldn't have said 'no.' Even if she didn't particularly like the song that was playing, she wouldn't be rude. She'd get up out of her chair and dance.

Today, something different is going on. My brother is a fashion designer. I recently went to a party after one of his fashion shows, and was dancing with one of his models from the show. Remember now that when Barry is on the dance floor, he is in his element. Nothing pretty much I'd rather do than dance to a good song–or even a mediocre one. So there I am, dancing with this model, when out of nowhere one of her friends–another female who had also been working the fashion show–came over and took away my dance partner.

"Wait a minute!" I called out. "What are you doing?" as the two ladies started off. I told them plainly, "That was rude." The friend chimed in, saying, "Well, *we* wanted to dance." I replied, "Well, that's fine, but *we* were *already* dancing." I added, "If you were out there dancing with a man, I wouldn't come and pull your man away so I could dance with *him*." I was making a joke to prove my point, but it didn't seem to register with these ladies. They continued their exit, with the friend telling me, "Well, we're girls–it's not the same thing." Tell me.

That happened in Melbourne, Florida. Fast forward to the cruise I was just on. Uncle Barry's back on the dance floor, dancing with another young lady when again, out of nowhere, this young lady's girlfriend steps in front of me and starts dancing with my dance partner. I'm dumbfounded, thinking, "What *is* this? This is so *strange*." I want you all to know that in all cases, I was dancing as I usually do–just to get my little exercise in and enjoy myself. Nothing provocative at all.

I've found this is happening all over place. The next time, it was in Atlanta. It's the Memorial Day brunch at Negril Village, 30 North Avenue Northeast in midtown Atlanta. Great Caribbean food. I'm dancing with a lady and the next thing I know, her friend is pulling her away. I go, "Whoa-whoa-whoa-whoa-whoa! (Actually, there might have been six "Whoa's.") Why are you doing that?!" The puller answered, "Oh, I have to go pee." I said, "*Oh*, you have to go *pee*? And *she* has to go *with you*?" She said, "Well, that's how girls *are*." You've got to be kidding me.

Well, they did their bathroom thing together, and after they came back, we talked and got a little more friendly and comfortable with each other. But I'm beginning to understand that when a woman sees her girlfriend dancing with a male, they put on their guard. Not sure why they'd need their guard up. After all, what's going to happen here? We're dancing in front of two hundred and fifty people at a nice restaurant. Am I going to murder her or assault her? I don't get it.

So after that, I said to myself, "Okay, I'm going to dance by myself for a little while." Part of my own dance routine is I have this white towel, because you can work up a good sweat on that dance floor if you're doing it correctly. When I have my towel, I always wave it. Previously when I was talking to these girls, one of them asked, "Can I hold your towel?" I said sure, and this lady stood up and waved the towel and she waved it good.

A little later, that group of four or five girls got up to dance, and I got up with them. However, when I started to dance with the young lady that had just been waving my towel around, she walked away and sat down. Again, I thought, "Hunh? What is going on here?" When I questioned her, she said, "Oh, I don't dance with men." This was bogus, because I'd just seen her dancing with another man before the group of them got up. Incredulous, I replied, "You don't?! But I just saw you with…" She cut me off, saying, "Oh well, that's my *friend*." Oh, okay.

The whole thing seemed strange. Now I'm back to dancing with myself, watching this lady talking to the guys she was with. I just kept on dancing, waving my white towel and the next thing I knew, the lady who had just sat down on me was back on her feet and dancing with me, and now she had one of her friends with her. So all the sudden, my score had gone from zero to two as one of them danced in front of me, the other behind. I wondered, "What in Heaven is going on here?" It was beginning to feel like the stuff that goes on at middle school dances, only we're all full-grown adults.

Then I happened to look over at the guys these two women had been sitting with, and guess what? They were both nodding in my direction, smiling and giving me the thumbs-up. Later, when I got over there, I asked them, "Did you *tell* them to dance with me?" They said, "Yeah, we did! Because all you wanted to do is dance with them, and we told them it wasn't right for them to act funny and sit down. You seemed like a good dude." We shook hands, high-fived and I thanked them. "That was a good move on your part," I said. "I'm new down here, and I don't understand the local customs."

What I've decided is that from now on, nobody's going to upset my plans. I'll take my shower, shave my head and put on my smell-good. I'll suit up, and if some young lady tells me no, I'm going on that dance floor and dancing with myself. What happens there, when people see you have the confidence to go out on that floor by yourself, they come to you. Life is funny. When you act confidently, like you don't even need them, they will start coming to you.

I also make it a rule that if I'm at a party, ask a young lady to dance and they throw shade on it or act distant, I will not ask them again. I wasn't going to ask those two again who ended up dancing with me after their gentlemen friends gave me the thumbs-up. But when they came up to me, they actually apologized. "We're sorry," one of them began as we started dancing. "Wow, man, y'all hurt my feelings," I told them, but I was laughing as I said it. "No," she went on, "that was our fault, and I came back and brought my girl with me." I turned around, and there was that same girl who had been waving my towel.

Later at that party, somebody gave me good advice. "You gotta remember that those women you were dancing with are thirty-five. Most people our age wouldn't treat you like that." Point taken. I'm better off at these social gatherings when I stick with my own age group. There's a natural tendency for me to go younger because I look and act younger than my real age. However, I'm learning that when I approach ladies my own age, things go a whole lot better.

I've also started employing what I call my 'senior strategy,' where I'll pick out somebody's grandmother and ask her to dance. If I spot one of these senior ladies sitting in her chair and moving to the music, I approach her. These ladies feel honored when I ask them to dance. I contrast that with the behavior of some young ladies who I ask to dance and they're snooty to me, like they think I want to marry them. And all I wanted was a dance.

I guess I have to own the fact that, as a sex, we men have helped create the problem. My observation is that men between the ages of twenty-five and thirty-five have no clue how to treat women. For them, it's *all* about sex; that's their jump-on point. Now I'm not saying that I don't want that also, but that's not all I want, and I don't lead with that. I'm interested in the whole package. So when I ask a woman to dance, I extend my fingers and gently pull her to the floor in a gentlemanly manner, like we used to do. And they are honored that somebody noticed them. The younger men's crowd, they think people notice them because they want to take them outside, get them in a car and have sex. (I'm exaggerating, of course–but you get my point.)

I'm a real people studier, and little by little I'm getting all this down to a science. I look at body language. At a party, I look for older women who are tapping their feet sitting at the table, because when asked to dance, they jump right up. I'm also learning that you have to be quick. I get caught up because I'm happy the DJ has my song on, but sometimes they cut it off. So when you hear the music, you have to grab somebody and not wait.

Men, particularly the younger ones, may be hung up on

sex. Ladies, on the other hand, are at least partly responsible for this.   Not too long ago, I was out dancing one night and Juvenile's song, *Back That Thang Up,* came on. The words to the song are very sexually-oriented, very degrading to women in my opinion. But guess who was out there dancing on the floor, 'backing it up' with their behinds in the air? Most of the women. I'm confused. You're a woman, you feel like all guys want from you is sex, and then you behave like that? Excuse me for sounding logical, but if you're a woman and *that's* your behavior–*backin' it up*–you should not be surprised when a guy comes over and acts like he wants you to *back that thing up.*

Whatever goes on in the Younger Generation, I'm going to remain a gentleman. I tell women I meet, "The one thing you need to know is that I'm going to be a gentleman first. I'll open the door for you. I'll take your hand as we're walking down a stairway. If you choose to think that means all I want is to have sex with you, then that's on you."

Things are all twisted now. It's not like when I grew up. Now it's backwards and upside down. There's a passage in Isaiah 5 that predicts this time we're living in, when people will say evil is good and good is evil. And I've had to close my ears to some of my buddies who tell me, "Man, you're too much of a gentleman! These women want you to call them 'bitch.'" That is not how my grandmother raised me. It's not my natural tune, and I am for sure not changing it to *Back That Thang Up*.

We all get misjudged. That's life. But women who judge me for a player have no idea. I haven't had sex in ten months. I have no desire to be jumping in and out of bed. I've done that before in my life, and I learned that's not how you mature. And for every woman who thinks that I *am* a player, I want to get this down in black and white: I'm a friendly dude and that's *it*. You have to look beyond my swagger.

I've had some hard lessons handed to me in my romantic life, but I'm not giving up. There are a lot of beautiful women out there, but because of the things guys have done, they have to be careful. Their girlfriends have to watch out for them. That's the way it has to be. I'll find which side of the boat to throw my net. What I have to do is carve out my little niche on the floor, wave my towel and move to the beat.

For now, all I wanna do is dance.

BARRY D. YOUNG

THE
LOVE BOAT

PEOPLE ASK ME why, when I want to go someplace, I just get in my car and go. There are two answers to that. One is that I love the solitude. It allows me to think on my own and listen to my music. The other is that when we get out there, we see the country as it really is. And that means we discover that racial conflict in America today is not what the media makes it out to be.

Interstate rest stops are in part proof of that, because they are a meeting place for every ethnicity and culture you can imagine. In these roadside microcosms of America, you'll find people being polite to each other, holding doors and allowing others to go ahead of themselves. Sadly, there are no news cameras there to document this courtesy. You only find the media where there are problems, not where people are showing their humanity.

I discovered the same thing recently on a cruise I took to the Caribbean. The staff required to run these big boats is enormous, and we were told that out ship's crew represented a hundred and sixty countries from around the globe. Thailand, Vietnam, the Philippines, India, Pakistan, Bangladesh, the Ukraine, and Latvia, just to name a few. Each member of the crew wore a name tag that also included the name of their home country.

Now if you believe all the media accounts, you would expect lot of tension on a ship staffed by so many people with different backgrounds and ideologies, given the amount of international turmoil that's splashed across the news every day. Yet on this cruise, from start to finish, I never heard one cross word from anyone. And where were the news cameras? Nowhere to be found.

I already know that the media prefers stories about bad things happening over good things. And even though I don't do politics, I see that in this election year with all the political rhetoric being thrown around out there, there's a need for stories that show most people are in fact getting along. Blacks and whites. Whites and Latinos. Blacks and Latinos. We're all basically getting along, and it's about time we stopped getting taken for a ride. During the cruise, one of the passengers—a black woman—had a party to celebrate her fiftieth birthday. On the dance floor at her party, there were people from at least twenty different countries. Everyone got along.

I've been interacting with people of other nationalities for a long time. As a train conductor, I did it for years. I developed a strategy of starting those interactions with a smile on my face. Start with a smile and the reaction is almost always positive. It also gets me over any feeling on the other person's part that I'm intimidating, because I know I'm a sizeable black man who likes to eat and has put on a little weight.

You may be thinking, "Okay, all those people working on that cruise ship have to get along with each other because their paychecks depend on it." But what I noticed is these people really treasure their jobs. Many come from smaller, developing nations and they were clearly happy to be working on this beautiful boat. I rarely saw any of them not working. They were always doing something.

Take our room steward, for example. He was from Phuket, one of the southern provinces of Thailand. This guy was so respectful. He had keys to our room so he could make sure things were ship-shape. If he was in the room when we returned, he would always give the room back to us and step out. But more than that, he made us feel welcome. Knowing I was a single man looking for my Superwoman, he'd ask, "Hey Barry, did you find a girlfriend yet?" And when I shook my head, he replied jokingly,

"You have to try harder!"

What I saw among all that diversity is how much we're all alike in so many ways. On board, there were a lot of families traveling together. Many had three generations represented–grandparents, parents and their children. I realized also that the people who worked on the boat had pride in their work because they, too, were representing their families. In a sense, they were working for the guests, but in a bigger sense they were working for their spouses and children who they left behind for several months at a time.

One of my favorite times on the cruise was when each night we sat down together for dinner. The dining room was filled with the sounds of people speaking many languages. I didn't understand most of it, but I watched as all these people chewed and swallowed their food like we did, blinked their eyes the same way we did, and all had an enjoyable time. We knew we had differences. But we accommodated each other for those differences, were courteous with each other and everything was smooth-sailing.

My experiences on dry land have shown me the same. Take my recent trip to Baltimore under the auspices of Music to Your Feet and a young lady named Denise Bryant. We set off on her party bus for a Maryland Dance and Crabfest–our black community on wheels headed for good times and those especially succulent crabs that only Baltimore can offer.

When we arrived, we were mostly waited on by people that didn't look like us. Largely white, and overwhelmingly friendly. It started with the waitresses. They picked up on our first names the first time they heard them, and it wasn't long before we were all on a first-name basis. We all came together as brothers and sisters, ignoring our obvious differences and focusing on fun and fellowship.

People watching would have seen me and one of my newfound Baltimore friends as the ultimate Odd Couple. I've already described myself, so I don't need to do that again. But picture me next to my short-statured, crusty looking white brother, watching the Orioles play the Yankees. No race riot. Only a couple of guys talking about and watching the Great American Pastime. Another picture of tolerance and humanity worth noticing but too insignificant for media coverage.

The longer I live, the more I understand the meaning of Proverbs 18:24: "A man who has friends must himself be friendly." It takes reaching outside yourself to learn how fast strangers can become friends, and friends become brothers. This is my testimony. I've seen it work hundreds of times in my life, even with people who, on the surface, seem unapproachable–including God's Chosen People.

My former wife lives in Spring Valley, New York–an area

with a large population of Hasidic Jews. They never speak to her. They just look. And then look some more. I get confused, because I have a different idea of how God's Chosen People ought to behave. And I also have to be careful about making a blanket statement here. I'm speaking about my experience; others may differ. What I've found, however, is that when I speak to them, they speak back. When I abide by that Scripture and show myself as friendly, that's what I receive in return.

The truth is, we're all God's Chosen People. Some wear black coats and tall black hats. Some are big, bald-headed black men. Jews. Christians. Muslims. Buddhists. Black. White. Yellow. Red. Brown. All individuals, all struggling to find common ground. The only way we really find out is to reach out.

IF I CAN HELP
SOMEBODY

No WAY I COULD close out this book without giving my biggest shout-out of all to one of the most important woman in my life besides my grandmother, Helen Howcott Young (Lala). The one who saved me from going down the wrong road. The one who was tough on me when I didn't want it–but really needed it. The one who, more than any other person, I have to thank for turning me right-side up and making me the God-fearing man I am today. That woman is my Aunt Weezie.

She was the middle of three generations that made up our family. My cousins and I were the third generation, my grand-parents Poppie and Lala were the first. Aunt Weezie and my mother were the second. Weezie was our disciplinarian, without a doubt. I get a kick out of it now. When I disciplined my own kids, they'd ask me, "Daddy, why do you have to raise your voice? Why do you have to say it so many times?" And I say, "Because I've already told you eighty million times." That's the same line Aunt Weezie used to give me.

Those flashbacks to how she disciplined helped me understand Weezie's methods. She wasn't exaggerating; she *had* told us eighty million times not to do something. The hard part for her was having to deal with us after we didn't listen, when we'd done things our way and then had to come back to her for her help.

That realization also helped me understand her ministry better. In the pulpit, Weezie would *preach*. And preach. And preach some more. As a teenager, I asked the same question my kids asked me. "Aunt Weezie, why do you keep saying the same things over and over again?" She knew the answer. She repeated herself because she knew she'd be seeing a lot of us shame-faced and on the back end of things when we hadn't listened to her and had gotten in trouble.

In a world with plenty of shady characters, Weezie's character was spotless. She was a Christian who walked upright, no exceptions. In all those years, I never saw her do anything that caused me to question the integrity of what she preached, her love for her family or her dedication to her ministry.

There are really two sides to Weezie's personality. People

who didn't know her outside the pulpit got only one. She was a fiery preacher who told it like it is. That they knew. What they didn't always know was this was her role. When you're a pastor, you have to come out strong in the pulpit. It's the job God gave you.

Outside the church, she was a lot of fun. When I joke with her now, she'll look at me first with amazement, then she just starts laughing. I believe part of our bond is that when she was a teenager, she was mischievous like me. In Greenburgh, back in the day, Weezie had been a gang leader. Her gang, The Eaglettes, was more about dressing nice and throwing parties than swinging chains. Still, she wouldn't take stuff from anybody. I've heard stories.

The only man who could ever tell her what to do was her father, my grandfather Poppie. I'm trying to inherit Poppie's role now. Weezie has moved into assisted living in Atlanta, and taking care of her is partly my responsibility. "There's only one man you ever listened to," I say, "and that was Poppie. He's gone now, so guess who's in charge?" I poke myself on the nose. She'll glare at me, frown and then bust out laughing. "You're not running the show–I'm running it," I tell her. More laughter.

I talk to Weezie any way I want. It's our banter, and also our bond. It's not disrespectful but it is bold, and that's the only way she likes it. You cannot come to her like a mouse. Even now, at eighty years old, if you come to her timidly she will walk her heels all over you.

My plan is to move to Atlanta to be close to Weezie for whatever time God has left for her here. I owe her that because she never gave up on me. If I needed money, she would fuss, but would end up giving it to me. She'd still tell me, for the eighty millionth time, "If you'd done it like I *told* you, you wouldn't have this problem." But that declaration was always followed by, "How much do you need?" The irony for me now is the lessons she taught me that I hated most at the time are the ones I appreciate the most today. That appreciation makes me want to give back to her. Now's my time to show and prove.

When I get to Atlanta, my ministry to her is to get her out a couple of times a week. It gives her something to look forward to beyond the routine of assisted living. I take her out for four hours at a time. When we're done, she's exhausted and says, "Okay, Barry, I'm ready to go back." I'm still not used to hearing her say that, because all her life she was on the go. Poppie called her 'The Roadrunner,' because Weezie was always running somewhere–off to preach in Ohio, or Chicago or places in the South.

We talk about those days to jog her memory now, because as a boy I often went with her. For me, it was quite an adventure. We flew together on Pan Am in the days when you still had to walk across the tarmac and up the stairs to board the plane. Even though technically she was my aunt and I was her *sister's* son, I was a son to her.

Aunt Weezie was serving up tough love long before anybody even called it that. Yes, she might be fussing at you. But you'd better believe that if she was spending her valuable time fussing at you, it was because she loved you. I get that now, and I appreciate it. I honestly don't know where I'd be today without her. I'd been in trouble before, minor scrapes when I was younger. Thank God that trouble never got any deeper. That was Weezie's doing.

They say wisdom comes with age. Not always true, but it is in Weezie's case. She has this way of looking at me like I'm crazy. Then she'll burst out laughing and say four little words that are worth a whole page from most people. More and more, I hear God speaking through her. He probably always has. I just never had the ears to hear it. Check Matthew 11:15.

Age hasn't dampened Weezie's spirit. Sometimes I'll holler, "Aunt Weezie, when are you going to stop chastising me?! I'm over fifty years old now!" Calmly, she explains it to me. "Well, Barry," she says, "you're still the same number of years younger than me as you were when you were born." In other words, she's still got all those years on me. Therefore, her license to chastise has not expired.

I'm amazed today to see what God has put in my heart

through Aunt Weezie. I remember all the people she helped, too—many who could never pay her back. When I speak to them, they always say, "Man, if it wasn't for your aunt..." It's a familiar line, because that's my line, too.

I believe you should give flowers to people while they're still living. When Weezie goes on to be with the Lord, a lot of people will come forward to thank her. "Aunt Weezie, if it wasn't for you..." is a phrase I try to work into every conversation I have with her. She smiles and says, "Thank you." She doesn't really know what to say to these accolades, because in spite of her pulpit personae, she's a very humble lady.

I'm leaving you with two photos of her before we close the album. The first is Weezie The Disciplinarian. Eight-year-old versions of Cousin Earl and myself are gripping the edge of the bathtub as she wails on us. Earl and I were often together in this posture, but I have the distinction of being the most frequent receiver of Aunt Weezie's 'correction sessions.' The second is of she and I crossing the tarmac to board a Pan Am flight to Toledo. Me and my other mother, The Roadrunner.

Thanks, Weezie. Words can't express it. Let the church say, Amen!"

TURN THAT FROWN
UPSIDE DOWN

"WHAT ARE YOU GOING TO DO when you *retire*, Barry?" I get that a lot from people since hanging up my conductors hat. The person asking me the question usually wears a frown, like from their point of view my life must be over. My answer to that question has been, "I'm going to do whatever I want." I think about that frown face sometimes when I'm traveling. Are they envious? I waited thirty-three years to travel, and now I'm doing it. Retirement is not a death sentence.

Maybe they look at it differently. I remember a guy I worked with on the railroad. He was about sixty, and not more than two weeks after he retired he was dead. It's sobering. How can a person work for fifty years, retire and then drop dead? Aunt Weezie used to preach the reality of death. "If you don't get your life together," she'd say, "one day you're gonna wake up *dead*." She didn't play. It may have sounded harsh, but many people got turned around right by her saying that.

That "What are you going to do…?" question comes up for me almost every day. It flashes in my mind. At first, I wasn't quite sure what the answer was. I sat in my house and was bored. Then I hit the road. I set my GPS on destinations where there were people I wanted to see. I have a long list. When you look at it right, retirement should be my reward for the almost nine thousand days I spent on the job, and to some degree for the things you have to put up with in a job where you're serving the public, the supervisors you have to answer to and could never speak your mind to and all the rest.

My bucket list isn't only travel. I'm currently working on a short film with a filmmaker from my old neighborhood. I said that I want to launch my own Internet radio station. I've started a car transporting service. I want to open an upscale men's hat shop in Atlanta. I'm writing this book. If you can catch me, I'll give you the full list. Just be prepared to stay a while.

Before I started at the railroad, I was interested in drawing. I used that talent to court young ladies. When I'd give a woman flowers, I'd draw little stick figures on the card. Now I have in mind a line of long-sleeve T-shirts and hoodies based on those nicknames I used to give my train riders.

My point is that retirement is your time to dream. Meet new people. Explore. Do all those things you dreamed about but couldn't because you were locked into the world of work. I'm not ungrateful for that work; it's how the bread got buttered for me and my family. I now thank God that after that long, long train ride, butter is no longer an issue.

You should have two retirement dates in your head. One is the day when the company says you *can* retire, and the other is the date you tell yourself. Have a plan. A plan can help you keep going through those days on the job when you want to overreact. It's easy to forget the reward that's out there. The last year was rough for me, and sometimes I had to vent to my coworkers or my regulars. However, they steadied me. "Hey Barry," they'd tell me, "you only have eight months to go. Just *chill*." That carried me through. Also, knowing there was an endgame for me and that it was going to be fun took away the fear that life would end at retirement.

Now a word about butter. Everybody needs a pension. If your employer doesn't offer one, get it for yourself. The reason I don't have to worry about getting my bread buttered any more is that I saved for this retirement for a long time. Don't wait thirty years and then wonder how you're going to retire. Feed your 401K. It's your nugget. It's one of the things you're working for. If you're faithful to it, it will grow.

Having retired at 55 years of age, you know I'm a fan of re-tiring as soon as you can. There's too much life out there to be had that you'll never get to if you work until you drop. I have children and grandchildren. Last time I saw them, when I was still working, it was for two days because I had to be back to work on Monday. Now I can stay for two weeks. Why do we give our employer our whole life? I understand 'giving;' it's a give-and-take world. But I also understand Aunt Weezie. One day we could also wake up dead.

I chose to retire early. There was even a point where, before so many months had passed, I could have changed my mind and gone back. I remember how it felt when that time came and went. Still, I have no regrets. I do miss those people I got to meet daily from all walks of life. In my heart, I know I will see some of them again. I'll be driving down the road, stop at a rest stop, and some guy will come up and say, "Wait a minute... weren't you my conductor up in New York?" As far as rewards in retirement go, that's worth as much as anything I ever put in my 401K.

Retirement has already taught me a few things. I realize now how blessed I was to have a job I really liked, where I was able to earn enough money to be comfortable when I left it. That's not the same for everyone. I know people making so little they don't even have the money to get a car right now. By God's grace I never forget how lucky I am. I know it could have gone much differently for me. Nothing I have is taken for granted.

Having a bucket list is one thing, and I intend to do my best to knock off every item on that list. But having the right attitude in retirement is also essential. For me, every day I'm going to live, laugh, love, praise God and dance like nobody's watching. I don't even care any more if people are watching. If they hate on me, that's fine. I *know* I can dance.

There's a prayer I say every morning. I don't say my prayers at night any more. At night, I end up watching TV and sometimes fall asleep after too much *Perry Mason*. I say this prayer in the morning, because that's when I struggle. It usually goes something like this:

Okay, God, I want to do this day right.
Thank You for waking me up.
Help me to do the things You want.
Help me not to do the things we don't want.
I give glory, honor and praise to Your Name.
Thank You. Amen.

Two more things on the bucket list before we close out. I want to dance in all fifty states of the Union. I also want to attend the TCM Classic Film Festival they have in Hollywood every year. I love black and white movies, and I am literally a Lionel

Barrymore, Humphrey Bogart and Robert Mitchum freak.

Don't get the impression it's all been frowns. I've gotten my share of laughs, too. Even before I left the railroad, passengers would tell me, "Barry, you're hilarious! You should do comedy!" And I'd reply, "Yeah, I've been thinking about doing it in my retirement. I could do stand up... until they tell me to sit down." (Ba-da-boom.)

A F T E R W O R D

AUTHOR'S NOTE: Anybody who has known me for a minute knows that I like to talk. The women in my family might even say I always need to have the last word. In this case, however, I'm giving the last word in my book to my oldest daughter, Tachelle. What follows is a speech she wrote for class in her freshman year at Howard University. This speech is one of my most treasured things. As you'll read, she really lets Daddy have it–but in a good way.   – B.D.Y.

To my fellow classmates, Ms. Ravisee and Dr. Fleet:

Good morning! Thank you for coming out to help me celebrate a very special individual, Mr. Barry Dean Young. I'm honored to have him here with us today. This is the man that's been instrumental in helping me become all that I am at this very moment. Not only is he my friend and mentor, but he's also my father. I realized I never took the time to express my gratitude for all he has done for me. Well, today is the day, Daddy. Today, I want you to know just how much you mean to me, and how different my life would be without you around.

Throughout my childhood, I listened to your continuous speeches about how your own father wasn't around. Back then, I saw it as a way of making us feel guilty. Now I see that it was much more than that. Not having your father around hurt you. But you were able to put aside those feelings and offer us love. That is commendable, and made you stronger than you think.

Though you had no one to learn from, you took on the challenge of parenting three daughters. I remember all the trips we took to Virginia, Florida, Detroit and New Orleans. Most kids don't travel much, but we did it so often we actually complained about it. You probably thought that we were ungrateful. Since then, we realized we took so much for granted. You cared about giving us those experiences. You instilled in us good parenting values that you had to learn on your own.

As early as age ten, I remember getting money for my birthday or other things. You always made me put at least a third of it in the bank–something I was never too happy about. I believed it was *my* money, and I should be able to do whatever I wanted with it. In the end, however, it paid off. I always had savings. In fact, I still save a third or more of what I receive.

When it came to making my bed, sometimes I'd be in a rush trying to catch the bus. On those days, the bed-making didn't happen. When I came home from school, there would be one of your infamous note cards on my pillow: TACHELLE,

PLEASE MAKE YOUR BED. I'd pick up the note, thinking, "Is he *really* that pressed?" But I would do it. Today, no matter how late I am for class, I always make my bed–even though I know there won't be any notes later.

I'm now a student at Howard University. I know I'm here because of my achievements, but you also had a lot to do with it. I hated being punished for not doing as well as you knew I was capable of. But it helped me develop goals for myself. Today I want to do well for you and Mommy, but even more for myself. This has made me both responsible and independent.

You always told me I could go to school wherever I wanted. You said not to worry about the cost, because you believed that I would be successful no matter where I was. You'll never know how much that meant to me, knowing that you trusted me enough not to limit my future to an idea of what we could afford.

Daddy, I know I never say this often enough, but I love you. I appreciate all that you've done to create a healthy family life for my sisters and me. You've given us your money, your time and your love. You made many sacrifices so we could have the best of everything–from that new winter coat to the college I dreamed of attending.

There aren't enough words to describe my gratitude, Daddy, so I won't even search for them. However, I will say that

I've learned so much from you—what I should look for in a man, and what I should be as a human being. Remember that I love you, and I always will. You've taken care of me in every instance. One day, I will gratefully take care of you.

From a Facebook post: October 29, 2015

I FELT I HAD TO SHARE THIS, because I think a few of you may know who I'm talking about. There is a conductor on the Metro-North Harlem line named Barry Young. And he is a breath of fresh air. Every trip, he walks through the aisle cracking jokes and giving everyone nicknames like "slugger," "kiddo," or my particular favorite, "buttercup." This morning I got on the train (in not-the-best-mood-ever) but was instantly uplifted when I heard he was our conductor.

As usual he walked down the aisle checking tickets and doling out jokes and compliments. And, as usual, a car of tired, cranky commuters was changed to a group of pleasant adults. I guess they all needed that as much as I did. Coincidentally, today was his last day after 30+ years. As we pulled into Grand Central he read us a letter he wrote called "You People" about how much he loved his commuters and how, by simply reciprocating his good attitude we helped get him through some of the hardest times of his life. By giving him his stage and joking with him we helped make it easier for him to get out of bed in the morning when he didn't think he could. He continued to say that he loves us and will take us with him spiritually wherever he goes in life.

As everyone got off the train there wasn't a single person without a smile or even a few tears. This man is living proof of how strongly you can impact people just by being nice. If you have a good attitude and practice kindness, you will get exactly that back in your life. I don't take the same train every day, nor do I commute to the city every day. But of all the days and all the trains, I feel truly blessed to have been on that one and to have been one of those people to experience his good energy.

– *Karen Iallonardo*

The Red Velvet Seat

BARRY D. YOUNG